Global HR

Donna Deeprose

- Fast track route to managing human resources on a global scale

- Covers the key areas of global HR, from developing and compensating local and expatriate talent and working within local laws and customs to creating global HR strategy and succeeding as a strategic business partner

- Examples and lessons from some of the world's most successful businesses, including Nortel Networks, Matsushita, and Royal Dutch/Shell, and ideas from the smartest thinkers, including David Ulrich, Vladimir Pucik, Steve Kerr and Mike Losey

- Includes a glossary of key concepts and a comprehensive resources guide

PEOPLE

09.02

> EXPRESS EXEC. COM <
essential management thinking at your fingertips

The right of Donna Deeprose to be identified as the author of this work has been asserted in accordance with the Copyright, Designs and Patents Act 1988

First published 2002 by
Capstone Publishing (a Wiley company)
8 Newtec Place
Magdalen Road
Oxford OX4 1RE
United Kingdom
http://www.capstoneideas.com

CIP catalogue records for this book are available from the British Library and the US Library of Congress

ISBN 1-84112-343-9

Printed and bound in Great Britain

This book is printed on acid-free paper

Substantial discounts on bulk quantities of Capstone books are available to corporations, professional associations and other organizations. Please contact Capstone for more details on +44 (0)1865 798 623 or (fax) +44 (0)1865 240 941 or (e-mail) info@wiley-capstone.co.uk

Contents

Introduction to
ExpressExec

ExpressExec is 3 million words of the latest management thinking compiled into 10 modules. Each module contains 10 individual titles forming a comprehensive resource of current business practice written by leading practitioners in their field. From brand management to balanced scorecard, ExpressExec enables you to grasp the key concepts behind each subject and implement the theory immediately. Each of the 100 titles is available in print and electronic formats.

Through the ExpressExec.com Website you will discover that you can access the complete resource in a number of ways:

» printed books or e-books;
» e-content – PDF or XML (for licensed syndication) adding value to an intranet or Internet site;
» a corporate e-learning/knowledge management solution providing a cost-effective platform for developing skills and sharing knowledge within an organization;
» bespoke delivery – tailored solutions to solve your need.

Why not visit www.expressexec.com and register for free key management briefings, a monthly newsletter and interactive skills checklists. Share your ideas about ExpressExec and your thoughts about business today.

Please contact elound@wiley-capstone.co.uk for more information.

Introduction

» The paradox in "thinking globally, acting locally"
» HR's acceptance as a strategic business partner
» HR's future: smaller with more impact.

The words "global human resources" are so loaded with tension, it's amazing they don't spring right off the page.

The only way to examine the function is to look at the opposing forces, pushing and pulling at every strategy, every decision, every action taken in the name of HR in enterprises that operate beyond their home country borders.

Start with the first word, "global." Just think about the inherent conflict in the popular exhortation: "think globally, act locally." Consider this example: from a business perspective, it's thinking globally to sell your product on the Internet. The acting locally component is the tough part: matching what you feature online with regional preferences, and delivering promptly anywhere in the world.

From an HR point of view, the global/local alignment may be even more discordant. It's thinking globally to staff a new operation anywhere in the world with the best skilled, most experienced people, wherever they come from. Acting locally might require you to use a government-mandated or strongly preferred percentage of locals. It may be thinking globally to develop an incentive plan, including stock options, for personnel around the world. Acting locally, you may confront different expectations for compensation, or tax laws regarding foreign investments that complicate executing your plan.

Or acting locally, your company may have smashed the glass ceiling that held women back from reaching the highest levels in the organization. Thinking it's high time to make that practice global, you may run smack into locally legal, deeply-held biases toward women executives that can paralyze them in some countries in the world.

Here's a different kind of example: you could say that Nike and Kathie Lee Gifford's sportswear concern were thinking globally and acting locally when they located their assembly plants in low-cost areas and paid workers the going wage. But that didn't relieve the tension when global watchdog groups targeted them for labor practices that looked like exploitation by the standards of developed countries.

It's a small world alright, but not so small that local actions won't keep right on conflicting with global thinking for some time to come.

THE PROPER ROLE OF HUMAN RESOURCES

So the word "global" throbs with tension. The words "human resources" don't rest easily either. The strain results from the movement in more and more organizations to raise the function out of its transactional origins and into a role of strategic business partner. Few companies have departments they call Personnel anymore; over the past 25 years that label has been shed in favor of the more strategic sounding Human Resources. But in the beginning the change was more semantic than meaningful. The department went on screening job candidates, keeping employment records, and administering compensation and benefits plans. Over time, however, as companies began to issue values statements that invariably declared people to be "our most valuable resource," some organizations recognized the importance of making that most valuable resource an important component of strategic planning. If anything, this movement is most striking in global enterprises where adapting global thinking to local labor practices and cultural realities can make or break an operation.

At the same time as the strategic role of HR grows, the transactional side is increasingly being automated. Employees go online these days to update their personal records or to examine their benefits alternatives and make their choices, rather than checking with a benefits administrator. Other personnel administrative tasks are also going the electronic route.

What all this means, predicts author, consultant, and educator David Ulrich, who has been listed by *Business Week* as one of the world's top ten educators in management and the top educator in human resources, is that in the next five-ten years HR will get a lot smaller and have a lot more impact.

The people with the most impact will be those who can manage the tension.

Definition of Terms

» Two ways to define global human resources
» What the most global companies do differently
» Stages of internationalization.

There are two definitions of global human resources. The first is broad, and describes the job of human resources professionals in any organization with operations outside its home country. The second is more exclusive, and for many it is more aspirational than descriptive of the current situation. It is reserved for the HR function in those enterprises – and there is only a handful – deemed truly global because they have not only crossed country borders, but transcended them. Their view of the world is almost totally devoid of home country biases. This second definition of global human resources is less about what HR professionals do and more about how they do it.

THE INCLUSIVE DEFINITION

Defined most broadly, global human resources is the performance of the traditional HR functions of staffing, compensation/benefits, training and development, performance management, and labor relations, and the newly emerging one of being a strategic business partner within an organization that operates internationally.

Of course, that doesn't begin to describe the complexity of the field or to target what differentiates international human resources managers from their domestic counterparts. For one thing, human resource professionals in multinational firms perform activities, such as those below, that are not required by their counterparts who operate only domestically.

» *Managing international relocation for expatriates and their families*, made complicated by visa/immigration requirements, language problems, and cultural hurdles.
» *Providing a variety of services for relocating employees and their families.* These range from arranging for taxation counseling and language lessons, to handling housing and school arrangements, health care services, and family support. In fact, in the global arena, the HR function usually gets much more involved with employees' personal lives than either employer or employee would be comfortable with at home.
» *Building close relationships with governments of other countries where the company operates.* Without these relationships it can be very difficult to obtain visas, work permits, and other necessary

documentation, and to navigate through local labor laws and regulations.[1]

But not only additional tasks make global HR different. In the international playing field, the traditional activities take on more complexity. HR professionals in domestic companies need to contend with social security regulations, labor laws and taxation requirements of just one national government. HR professionals in multinational enterprises may have to design and administer programs that work for employees traveling to and from several countries with conflicting laws and requirements. They need to contend not only with legal differences but cultural ones too – and be able to differentiate between the two.

When, for example, does one culture's expectations of gift-giving run afoul of another country's definition of a bribe? How do you reconcile behaviors that are approved in one country but frowned on in another? Profiled in the "Global HR Leaders Agenda" Steve Kerr, chief learning officer at Goldman Sachs (formerly vice president of General Electric), gives a good example:

"... although it is politically incorrect to favor a friend or family member for a potential vacancy in the US, in some countries, especially in the Far East or Latin America, it's the done thing."[2]

Human resources professionals who approach the international playing field with a domestic mindset run a minefield of conflicting expectations, behaviors, and regulations.

THE EXCLUSIVE DEFINITION

The word "global" is ubiquitous in the business world these days. Type "global business" into the Google search engine on the World Wide Web and you'll get 250,000 matches. But many people don't toss it around that lightly. They save it for enterprises where the concepts of parent country and foreign operations have dimmed and merged into one world view. It's an ideal, perhaps. One company that has come closest to reaching it is Royal/Dutch Shell. So John Hofmeister, Shell's group HR director, has excellent credentials for defining global human resources within this narrower domain. In an interview with the author he explains it in this way:

> "A really global company has to be broader culturally than its dominant national country of origin. If you think about your company in terms of your headquarters' national culture, the issues of globality will never really be addressed. There are several distinctive characteristics of what being global means."

> "First is the ability to attract, retain, and develop staff from all over the world, who can then rise to the top and participate in executive decision making. Those decisions then reflect their cultural backgrounds and their international perspectives. More than 50% of our top 200 executives come from countries all over the world, other than the three top countries in which we do business: the Netherlands, the UK and the US."

> "Second is the extent to which staff from all over the world are taking assignments all over the world. We have 6000 people living outside their home country. This is to ensure that we have a talent pipeline, so that as people progress in their careers they are never held back because of not having enough international experience."

> "Third would be the extent to which a company's policies are independent of a central national bias, so they are applicable everywhere. At Shell, we only have four company policies:"

» Our business principles policy: no matter where we operate in the world, we live according to one policy of business: no bribes, no conflict of interest, no violations of national rules of whatever country we operate in.
» Our policy on health, safety, and environment, which sets worldwide standards equal to the most vigorous HSE rules of any country in the world.
» Our policy on sustainable development: we make certain commitments to our stakeholders about what we do as a company in the area of sustainable development.
» Our policy on diversity: we have a written policy which stakes out certain basic provisions for our people all over the world. It's built around a sense of inclusiveness, fairness, justice, and

problem-solving. One of the key things is that in any country of the world people have a mechanism by which they can complain safely about their treatment. It's the safety aspect that is key.

"So I think what global HR means to me is maintaining flexibility and adaptability that can easily override home country bias. Technically we have our official headquarters in the Netherlands and in the UK, but the labor laws or the cultures of those countries affect only a small part of Shell, so we have a very different mindset when it comes to creating and implementing policy."

DEFINING THE ROAD TO GLOBAL

If we accept the more exclusive definition of "global", there are a number of stages that companies usually go through to get there. And there are hundreds of multinational enterprises that operate successfully at a stage short of that global ideal and may not even aspire to it. At each stage there are somewhat different "global" responsibilities for the HR department.

» *Stage 1 Pre-international*. The company operates only domestically, making and selling its product in its home country.
» *Stage 2 Exporting*. The company expands its market, selling its product in other countries. International contact is primarily through the marketing department. HR's international involvement is still limited.
» *Stage 3 Overseas production*. Rather than exporting, the company decides to assemble or manufacture its product abroad to serve its international markets. For the most part, managers of the local operations will be expatriates from the parent country. At this stage, corporate HR becomes involved in providing services for expatriates as well as for local employees to some degree. The tasks and complexities described under the first definition of "global" begin to kick in.
» *Stage 4 Multinational operations*. At this stage, the company's foreign operations probably account for half or more of its sales and employment.[3] Operations of this magnitude require a more

sophisticated structure. Companies may divide their international operations into regions, with a regional headquarters for each; or they may organize globally along product lines. Either way, HR functions will be divided between local HR and regional/global HR departments, with a delicate and probably shifting balance between the two as the company strives for consistency among the HR policies of its various operations, while accommodating local practices and regulations. In one international financial services firm, for example, officers and directors from around the world gather in Europe for intensive management training, while training and development departments in local subsidiaries create complementary programs for managers at lower levels.

The need to provide relocation services and training for globe-trotting employees expands. Now the travel begins to go both ways. Not only do more managers move into foreign operations but foreign employees may relocate to the home country for two-to-three year stints at headquarters. These people are often called *inpatriates*, and their relocation raises most of the same issues that expatriates face. And a new group of employees begins to appear, people who move from one subsidiary operation to another, who originate from neither the parent country nor the host country where they currently work. So HR professionals serve a triumvirate of:

» parent country nationals, either at home or abroad;
» host country nationals, in their local operations or as inpatriates; and
» third country nationals, working in operations that are in neither their country of origin nor the parent country.

Many of the world's largest multinational enterprises operate around the world at this stage of internationalization.

» *Stage 5 Transnational or truly global operations.* Transnational enterprises view the world not as a collection of national or regional markets but as one market. They produce wherever costs are lowest and quality highest and deliver their good and services wherever demand is highest. They seek resources – money, technology, people – wherever the best can be found (defining "best" as they see fit, whether that is best absolute quality or best value per cost). Even the concept of parent country diminishes. Their "headquarters" may be in their country of origin, may have relocated elsewhere, or may be split up into autonomous units.

For the HR function in a transnational enterprise or one developing toward this stage, balancing worldwide consistency and equity with increasing local control requires even more sophistication. While the business of the enterprise may be truly global, with decentralized decision making, there are still central, corporate values that need to be maintained in HR programs and services around the world. More than ever, the HR function still needs to deal with expectations and cultural characteristics of its three-fold clientele and the regulations and business practices that characterize all its host governments.[4]

For the most part, this book will take a broad view of the term "global human resources" to cover the responsibilities, tasks, and the aspirations of human resources professionals at every stage along the way to true globalization.

NOTES

1 Dowling, P.J., Welch, D.E., & Schuler, R.S. (1999) *International Human Resource Management: Managing People in a Multinational Context*. South-Western, Cincinnati, OH.
2 "Global HR Leaders Agenda," based on a survey done by Cendant International Assignment Services in association with HR World and the International Institute of Human Resources (now SHRM Global Forum). Found at www.shrmglobal.org/publications/hrworld/leaders.htm.
3 Briscoe, D.R. (1995) *International Human Resource Management*. Prentice Hall, Paramus, NJ.
4 The stages are adapted from a model introduced in Johanson, J. & Vahlne, J.E. (1977) "The Internationalization Process of the Film," *Journal of International Business Studies*, Spring/Summer.

Evolution

» The post WWII explosion of international operations
» The push/pull between central and local control
» Personnel's evolution into human resources
» The top issues for global HR today.

To describe the evolution of global human resources, one has to merge two stories. The first tells of the development of human resources management from its origins in personnel administration. The other describes the growing globalization of companies that sought originally, not to change their character, but merely to expand their markets or find more cost-efficient production locations.

Combined, it's the story of how the HR function has been striving to transcend its image as a record-keeping, policy-policing nuisance and emerge as a strategic business partner in international organizations where the application of centralized control has been swinging on a divergence/convergence pendulum for decades.

IN THE BEGINNING ...

Some scholars pinpoint 1920 as the year the human resource function was born,[1] perhaps because that year brought the publication of the discipline's first textbook, entitled *Personnel Administration*.[2] Under that umbrella title, the book laid out prevailing practices in employment, compensation, discipline, and other topics related to employees. Yet companies were obviously handling personnel issues before the 1920s, often through an office called the employment management department. A 1903 article in *The Engineering Magazine* described the need for an employment department devoted especially to issues concerning workers, aimed at forming a bond of trust between workers and management.[3] With the formalization of the personnel function in the 1920s, its purpose was "to get good employees and keep them."[4]

During those early years of HR (still called personnel administration), there were companies operating internationally, who needed to get good employees and keep them for facilities around the world. Many of these enterprises were European in origin, reacting to their limited domestic markets and evolving from their globe-spanning colonial pasts. Along with the Europeans were pioneering US firms, but their numbers were relatively few in comparison with what was to come. The real proliferation of companies investing in overseas operations began post World War II and exploded in the 1950s. So this chapter begins its examination of global HR with that decade.[5]

THE 1950S

Lured by post-war profit opportunities, US companies rushed offshore in the '50s. By the close of the decade US investment abroad was upwards of $10bn ($40bn if you count indirect as well as direct investment[6]). That represented over 50% of worldwide cross-border direct investment. Eighteen of the world's twenty largest corporations were headquartered in the United States.[7] The main story of global HR in the '50s lies in the practices of those US firms. Still new to operating internationally, their typical approach was to set up an international division, totally separate from corporate functions like personnel, finance, or marketing. Those in the international division became fast experts. Expatriate managers, still relatively few in number, negotiated their own compensation and incentive deals. Personnel policies and practices at the local level were determined and administered quite separately from their domestic counterparts.

Despite a frequent disregard for local customs by multinational corporations, many companies prided themselves on their fair treatment of local nationals. For example, among NCR's "basic principles" of foreign operations listed by the company's chairman in 1958 was: "We do not treat our overseas employees as step-children. We treat them exactly as we treat our people at home."[8] Still, then as now, one of the chief draws of overseas production was cheap labor. A spokesperson for the bicycle industry at that time pointed out that wage costs in the US were about $2.30 an hour compared with 60 to 70 cents in Germany.[9]

THE 1960S

As companies began to feel more sure of themselves in the international arena, headquarters control over international operations often tightened. The prevailing attitude became, "When in Rome, do as we do at home." Parent company hiring policies, performance standards, and management styles predominated. Upper management was most often a closed circle of parent company nationals.

Howard Perlmutter introduced a 3-style model to describe the relationships between headquarters and subsidiaries in international organizations.[10] Whole companies – or specific functions within companies – were defined as ethnocentric, polycentric, and geocentric.

In brief, ethnocentric enterprises were those characterized by strong parent country orientation and control. Key positions throughout the world were filled by people recruited and developed in the home country. Polycentric organizations hired and developed local nationals for key positions *in their own country* and gave subsidiaries a high level of independence, monitoring performance primarily with financial controls. Geocentric companies met what is still considered the global ideal, hiring and developing the best people anywhere in the world for key positions anywhere in the world and including heads of subsidiaries in the worldwide management team. Geocentric companies – few though they were – mastered the paradox of achieving a single worldwide strategy and developing a unified culture while responding to local interests and expectations. By their own admission, Perlmutter noted, all international firms of that time harbored at least pockets of ethnocentrism.

Throughout the personnel world, the hot new issue was management development. Until then the focus had been on training: teaching job-specific skills and patterns of behavior endorsed by the organization. Now, the personnel function extended its mandate. Training became training and development, expanded to include a range of experiential activities from job challenges to mentoring relationships, all aimed at maximizing each individual's potential for growth and readiness for promotion. At least that was the theory. In reality, personnel's control over experiences outside the classroom was usually limited.

Management development was more focused in personnel departments that managed another activity that was new to most of them: succession planning. Previously, personnel planning had concentrated on headcounts. Now attention turned to ensuring that skilled and effective people were ready to move into crucial management positions.[11]

In companies that operated internationally, overseas assignments became a crucial part of management development. Offshore operations were often used as training grounds for fast-trackers, who could count on coming home to important domestic positions. For the most part, however, those opportunities remained closed to nationals of the host countries, whose careers were still limited to local operations.

THE 1970S

Throughout the 1970s, subsidiary operations of international companies became increasingly localized. If you walked into the Mexico City office of a big multinational, you might be hard pressed to find an expatriate anywhere. At the same time, the filter created between subsidiary managers and corporate headquarters by the typical international division was dissolving. More and more, subsidiary managers, including personnel managers, dealt directly with their home office counterparts. On the one hand, that relationship raised the global/local tension, as the corporate personnel department strove to attain worldwide uniformity in personnel policies; while the local operations struggled with cultural and regulatory conditions the home office simply did not understand. From effective ways to motivate and reward people to local laws about hiring, vacations, and unions, there were myriad obstacles to smooth implementation abroad of policies geared to the home country. On the other hand, the direct contact between parent country and host country personnel departments began to overcome the knowledge gaps and break down the ethnocentric attitudes at headquarters.

While locals were taking over the management of established subsidiaries, that did not mean that the flow of expatriates subsided. There were always new overseas operations to start up and new functions or technologies to add to existing ones, providing plenty of opportunities for assignments abroad. During this period, another form of expatriate began to appear – third country nationals. It wasn't uncommon for a multinational enterprise to relocate a local manager with particular expertise to a subsidiary in a third country when that skill was needed. (It was, however, still uncommon to move such a person up into a headquarters position.) Now recruitment, compensation policies, relocation practices, and other functions took on an additional complication – reconciling the policies, practices and legal requirements of three or more countries instead of just two.

Performance appraisals for subsidiary managers assumed new complications. One question was: who appraises local managers who have dotted-line or direct reporting relationships to people far away? How managers of subsidiaries were appraised changed too, with increasing realization that financial success was affected by external factors such as currency fluctuations. International general managers – not just the finance people – had to become experts in managing cash flow, and that became a hot topic for the training and development function.

The international expansion brought so many challenges to personnel professionals that they began looking for opportunities to network and share information with their colleagues around the world. There were already organizations of personnel professionals in many countries. There were even regional groups such as the European Association for Personnel Management (EAPM). But there was no group that spanned the world until three existing organizations, EAPM, the Interamerican Foundation of Personnel Administration (FIDAP), and the American Society for Personnel Administration (now SHRM – the Society for Human Resource Management), co-operated to found the World Federation of Personnel Management Associations (WFPMA) in 1976. Its goal was "to aid the development and improve the effectiveness of professional people management all over the world." Since then, numerous national organizations have joined the federation.

Beginning in the '70s and gaining momentum in the decade that followed, the name Personnel Department began to disappear from corporate organization charts, replaced by Human Resources Department. While in many cases the name change was motivated more by fashion than values, it did mark the beginning of a philosophical shift. Personnel was a loose collection of functions relating to people. Human Resources looks at people as an organizational resource and focuses on maximizing that resource's contribution to the organization's success. It was not an overnight change, but the seed was sown.

In the United States, human resources departments got a new job, making equal opportunity and affirmative action work in their organizations. It entailed a combination of policy-making and policing, training, and changing people's minds and hearts. It expanded to combat sexism, ageism, and freedom from harassing behavior. Within the next decades, it would impact human resources policies and practices around the world.

THE 1980S

While cultures and employee expectations varied from country to country, by the 1980s they were also changing everywhere, so there was a constant learning curve for both host country and parent company managers. Mike Losey, former president and CEO of SHRM and a past president of WFPMA, recalls visiting a UK subsidiary of a US company to check out a new pension plan. He found a provision for a *widow*'s benefit. He recommended changing the provision to read "spouse's benefit," pointing out that the existing wording would be illegal in the United States. The locals argued that it wasn't illegal in the UK and that every company had a widow's benefit in its pension plan. Knowing the company employed women scientists, Losey was certain the provision would be challenged sooner or later, but he couldn't budge the plan's developers. Four weeks later, he recalls, he got a frantic call from London. "Mike," he heard, "we've got a riot on our hands. Can we tell them it's a printer's error?"

One of the hottest issues for both domestic and international HR in the '80s was leadership development. For international companies it held a double promise. The first was to instill managers with a set of newly defined leadership skills – previously assumed to be innate, not learnable. Beyond that, it promised a forum to communicate a shared vision, set of values, and strategic goals to managers from around the world and to prepare managers to translate those things meaningfully within their local environments.

Corporate universities began to pop up all over. The model was General Electric's corporate business school in Crotonville, NY, which had been a highly respected corporate learning institution for decades. But, from about 1982, it became a medium not only for teaching business skills, but for implementing and spreading the culture change and new initiatives envisioned by chairman Jack Welch.

THE 1990S

By the 1990s, the proportion of US-based multinationals had changed dramatically. In the middle of the decade, just eight of the world's twenty largest corporations were headquartered in the United States.[12] The flow of investment into the United States soared, often through acquisitions by foreign companies. Thus you could be working for Paramount Pictures one day and for Sony the next, or for Chrysler and then DaimlerChrysler. Even at the very American institution, the Equitable Life Assurance Society of the United States, people suddenly found themselves working for AXA, the French-based multinational.

Now the culture shock was happening in the opposite direction as managers from other countries struggled with understanding American labor laws and attitudes while choosing the best schools for their transplanted children. And HR professionals in the acquired companies, whose previous experience was domestic only, now had to translate America for their new bosses while implementing unfamiliar policies and programs among American employees.

Technology advances presented unprecedented opportunities and unforeseen problems. Internet technology provided worldwide access to human resources information systems; employees could manage their own benefits programs online. But, as Dave Ulrich, a leading HR consultant, educator, and author, tells it, "Some issues are trickier today because of the ready availability of information. For example, a company may have compensation policies that differ by country. In countries with high taxes, the company might pay less cash and more non-cash fringe benefits. Before, people in different countries would never talk to each other. Now they talk over the Internet and do comparison shopping. In the US, they ask, 'Why don't I get all the fringe benefits?' while the others are saying, 'Why don't I get the cash?'

As the unit responsible for staffing overseas subsidiaries, HR was confronting resistance to relocating among promising employees. A big obstacle arose in the form of dual career couples. The image of the stay-at-home wife packing up the household and following her husband abroad was ancient history by the 1990s, especially in US-based companies. Now potential expatriates were more typically married to people actively pursuing their own careers, which they were not eager to put on hold. Furthermore, expatriates themselves were finding that the move could forestall, not advance their own careers. After a stint abroad, repatriates were coming home to discover they'd been passed over and relegated to the sidelines.

On the positive side, the long-pursued goal among HR professionals to play a meaningful role in developing business strategy finally began to happen. As vice president of human resources for Hexel Corporation in the late '90s Lynn Brown, who is now a consultant, was part of a management team that developed strategy for the company, then took the message on the road internationally. "We did five road shows in the US," she recalls, "and then we went to England, France, and

Belgium. First the COO presented the overall plan, and then the key leaders described how their units' business plans complemented the company one. Then we had the audience dialogue with us in a two-way communication process: What did you hear? What's your reaction? What questions do you have? At first we were afraid we couldn't do that in France, that it was too American a thing, but we found that in all European countries the process worked beautifully."

THE NEW CENTURY

In the early years of the new century and looking forward, global HR confronts a number of opportunities and challenges, most of them carrying over from the previous decade. Topping the list are these.

» Recruiting and retaining talent worldwide. This was number one as the century turned, but may be sliding onto the critical list as the economy remains in a slump.
» Developing leaders who are capable of thinking, inspiring, and acting in the global arena.
» Increasing HR's role as a strategic business partner.

Along the road to true globalism, the role of HR continues to mature and evolve.

A HALF CENTURY OF GLOBAL HR

The explosion of international commerce following World War II and the rebuilding of Europe and Japan led to the proliferation of multinational enterprises and, to support them, a new discipline of global human resources. Tracing its development by decades, here are some highlights.

1950s

» US-based companies expand offshore in unprecedented numbers. Their typical organizational model puts all foreign operations into an international division, isolating them from domestic personnel and other support functions.
» Expatriate compensation and rewards are negotiated case-by-case.

1960s

» For US-based international companies, headquarters control over local personnel policies tightens, often with a "when at Rome do as at home" approach, creating culture clashes.
» Management development and succession planning are hot HR issues, and assignments abroad are used as training grounds for executives.

1970s

» Increasingly, subsidiary operations are turned over to local management. Direct contact, unfiltered by the international division, increases between local and home country personnel functions.
» Third country nationals become a factor to deal with as companies moved managers from one subsidiary to another. For personnel departments, this means reconciling the policies, practices, and requirements of three or more countries instead of just two.
» Companies begin to change the name of the Personnel Department to Human Resources Department, recognizing people as an organizational resource – at least in theory.
» The World Federation of Personnel Management Associations is founded.

1980s

» Diversity concerns affect HR policies and practices in a growing number of countries.
» Leadership development becomes the number one issue, often based on the GE model.

1990s

» US-based companies' share of global commerce decreases.
» Internet technology totally changes communications, making information available instantly worldwide.
» Dual career couples and sidelined repatriates make overseas assignments less attractive, heightening the recruitment challenge.

» In many multinationals, HR professionals begin to make a serious appearance as strategic business partners.

2000s

» Challenges include recruiting and retaining talent, developing global leaders, and increasing HR's strategic role.

NOTES

1 Ferris, G.R. "Human Resources Management: Some New Directions," *Journal of Management*. May-June, 1999.

2 Tead, O. & Metcalf, H.C. (1920) *Personnel Administration*, McGraw-Hill, New York.

3 Described by Morgan Witzel (ed.) in "Introduction," *Human Resource Management*. (2000) Thoemmes Press, Bristol.

4 Ibid.

5 Much of the history of multinational enterprises in this chapter is derived from interviews with Ralph Diaz, former vice president of Business International Corporation, which was a pioneer in the field of international business journalism.

6 Clee, G.H. & di Scipio, A. "Creating a World Enterprise," *Harvard Business Review*. Nov-Dec, 1959.

7 Statement of Peter R. Merrill, Director, National Economic Consulting, PricewaterhouseCoopers LPP, on behalf of the National Foreign Trade Council, Inc. Testimony Before the House Committee on Ways and Means. Hearing on Impact of U.S. Tax Rules on International Competitiveness. June 30, 1999.

8 Clee and di Scipio at[6] above.

9 Ibid.

10 Perlmutter, H.V. "The Tortuous Evolution of the Multinational Corporation," *Columbia Journal of World Business*. Jan-Feb, 1969.

11 Mahoney, T.A. & Deckop, J.R., "Evolution of Concept and Practice in Personnel Administration/Human Resources Management (PA/HRM)," *1986 Yearly Review of Management of the Journal of Management*. Vol. 12, No. 2.

12 Merrill at[7] above.

The E-Dimension

» The current state of online recruiting
» What an ideal Web-based HRIS would do
» The surge in e-learning
» Administering benefits via the Internet
» The rise in virtual teams.

Virtual HR. Could it be? Could the quintessential touchy-feeling part of the enterprise be heading into faceless, impersonal cyberspace?

Well, not really. But never doubt this: whole chunks of traditional HR activities are going digital. Online recruiting has been a big part of the talent search for years now. Globally accessible human resource information systems (HRIS) are in the works, if not already functional, in many multinational organizations. E-learning is luring people out of classrooms and into the privacy of their own workstations or home offices. Employees are enrolling in benefit plans and updating their choices without calling on HR administrators for forms to fill out. E-mail and intranet discussion groups and chat rooms are linking people from locations around the world into virtual teams.

Your company is probably moving in all those directions. And if it's not, it soon will be. Depend upon it. The information superhighway may be strewn with the hulls of wrecked dotcoms, but they are barely obstructing the corporate racers zooming along it.

ONLINE RECRUITING

For recruiting on the Internet there are two ways to go, and they are not mutually exclusive. Most companies are doing both. The first way is through the big job-posting Websites. The second is recruiting from the company's own Website.

Internet recruiting is global by definition, since the sites are accessible from anywhere. That doesn't mean it makes sense for someone in Yellowknife, Northwest Territories, to post for a job in Sydney, Australia. So the major job sites such as Monster.com are establishing separate sites for jobs in various countries. Job seekers can search by region or country and employers can tailor their company profiles to appeal to potential recruits in different locations.

But companies don't depend upon the mass appeal of the giant job sites. They're taking a more direct approach, recruiting from their own Websites. While that approach may miss candidates who don't initially target the company as a potential employer, it weeds out some of those who blanket the world with their résumés. In a survey done in April 2001, Recruitsoft found that 88% of *Fortune's* Global 500 companies were recruiting on their corporate Websites.[1]

To make the most of corporate Website recruiting, Recruitsoft offers a list of best practices that include: link to careers section from homepage; information on benefits and culture; separate college recruiting section; job search by job category, location, and keyword; urgent jobs highlighted; complete job descriptions; one click to apply; pre-assessment tools for each job; choice of cut-and-paste form or résumé builder; attachment of formatted résumé; application automatically connected to a job position; anonymous application; e-mail to friend; job agent; profiling; reuse of candidate information for multiple applications; and online user feedback.[2]

One problem with online recruiting is that in one sense it works too well, prompting an overwhelming onslaught of responses, many of them useless. That is being addressed with filtering tools that weed out unqualified applicants and by online pre-employment testing. Companies are using assessment tools tailored to each job. Vendors are even developing tools automatically to translate assessments into different languages.

Even senior executive recruiting is moving online. Personal networking and traditional head-hunters haven't been replaced yet, but in the final four months of 2000, Monster.com registered more than 100,000 senior executives at its new ChiefMonster.com site,[3] which accepts only job seekers who meet qualifications requirements.

TAKING HRIS WORLDWIDE

Most companies don't yet have the human resource information system of their dreams, but they are working on it. The ideal is a Web-based system that stores each employee's job history, pay history, evaluations over the years, benefits choices, and education history. Employees anywhere could access their own records and HR professionals could use the database for internal recruitment and making training decisions. User-friendly interfaces would make it easy for the appropriate people to access the material and sort it in ways that contribute to their purposes. Screens would keep unauthorized people from seeing what was none of their business.

The technology is available, but building such a system is a tremendous undertaking. Just gathering all the information is daunting. And privacy restrictions in some countries affect what personal information can be stored and transported across borders – as in the UK, where the provisions of the 1998 Data Protection Act necessitate legal advice. European Union privacy laws block access to a great deal of personal information from outside the country in which it originates, but this restriction can be overcome with the written consent of each employee. There's an ongoing effort on the part of the US government to get the EU to loosen its restrictions to bring them closer to less stringent US privacy regulations, but most multinational companies find the best solution is to obtain employee permission.

Despite the difficulties, global companies are building accessible, flexible systems. Nortel Networks' HR professionals around the world have been able to access data on any employee for 15 years. Over those years the system was streamlined as the company moved from traditional mainframe systems to its current Web-based server infrastructure. What's new in the past few years, reports Martin Cozyn, vice president, global compensation and talent strategy, is the way information has converged, along with technology. "Our HR systems feed to a central data warehouse and also link with our non-HR systems," he explains. "For example, we can use HR data criteria to send mass e-mails from our communications systems to specific populations of employees around the world."

Royal Dutch/Shell has embarked on a four year, quarter-billion-dollar venture to build a data-rich system that will be as useful to individual employees wanting to verify their benefits as to organizational planners creating blueprints for new billion-dollar projects. (See "Royal Dutch/Shell's Global HR Strategy" in Chapter 7: In Practice.)

E-LEARNING

Imagine that you wanted to roll out a training program to thousands of employees all around the world. Just think about the logistics. Now imagine that you put it on the Internet, on a secure Website, for employees everywhere to access on their own schedules and complete at their own pace. Sounds like an ideal solution, doesn't it? No wonder the American Society of Training and Development (ASTD), in its *A Vision of E-Learning for America's Workforce*, reports that corporations are spending $1.2bn dollars on e-learning – and that's just US companies.[4] Companies around the world are following suit.

While it answers a number of problems for getting training into far-off places, e-learning confronts some challenges when it goes global. Language is one problem, although not an insurmountable one since, for many companies, English is the language of business anyway, and translation services can be called upon if necessary. But even a well-translated course won't work if all the examples and exercises are biased toward the parent-company culture. For Web-based training, there is often a bandwidth problem in developing countries, where slow Internet access can limit the use of learning-enhancing pictures, sound, and video segments.

Still, the growth of corporate e-learning continues. *Information Week* reports that at Cisco Systems 80% of the company's training is via the Internet, and that Arthur Andersen, the global accounting and consulting firm, uses global e-learning to train 77,000 employees in 83 countries.[5] Even McDonald's venerable Hamburger U in Oak Bridge, Illinois, is about to go virtual, according to *Fortune E-Learning*, which reports that in 2001 McDonalds will roll out an e-learning pilot program in four languages – English, Spanish, French, and Chinese – in North America, South America, Europe and the Pacific.[6] According to a benchmarking study done by Brandon Hall and Jacques LeCavalier, IBM now conducts 70% of its management training by e-learning.[7]

Just how companies are defining e-learning may vary. Some think strictly in terms of Web-based training, but usually it has a broader meaning. The ASTD report mentioned earlier defines e-learning broadly to include various forms of computer-based training, video confer-encing, satellite-delivered learning, and virtual education networks. But Web-based training, alone or in combination with other delivery systems, is where all the buzz is these days.

Nobody expects Web-based training to eliminate other forms. In fact, there seems to be a blending, rather than a differentiation of training delivery systems. A study of corporate e-learning by WR Hambrecht & Co. reports that "one of the hottest growth areas in online learning is the creation of Internet/intranet meeting places ('surrounds') for instructor-led classes to provide community, communication, and supplemental materials online."[8] The report asserts that "This new learning model facilitates studying, note-taking, class discussions, and 'catching up,' all of which enhance classroom instruction."

Apparently, the appeal of any-time, any-place learning is actually somewhat limited. The Hambrecht study finds that, after all, people want to interact while learning. The study predicts a surge in virtual classrooms once the technology is widely available and more user-friendly.

Despite the explosion of e-learning, the jury is still out regarding how well it can achieve one of its advocates' goals. In the e-learning industry, there's a strong push for tying e-learning endeavors to business strategy and making them accountable for measurable outcomes, results that can be confirmed on the job, not just by headcounts at courses. Of course, that's an issue that corporate classroom training has been struggling with for years, and there's no evidence yet that e-learning has a silver bullet.

BENEFITS ADMINISTRATION THE ESS WAY

One of the ways e-technology is relieving HR professionals of a load of drudge work is by moving benefits information, enrollment, and change processes onto interactive Websites. Brochures, paper forms, and the file cabinets full of employee benefits records are going the way of typewriters and carbon paper – artifacts of another age. In increasing numbers, companies are embracing online employee self-service (ESS) systems that allow employees to enroll in benefits programs and find out what their share of the cost will be; set up direct deposit of their paychecks; make changes in their employee records and benefits choices if they marry, divorce, or have children; change their tax-withholding status; sign up for training programs; and identify and apply for job opportunities.

But when you expand ESS to overseas operations, some complications do arise. Because benefits vary from country to country, online systems need a way to screen out data that doesn't apply. The last thing you'd want would be to force an employee in Germany or Denmark to wade through a list of health insurance options. Retirement plans vary too, as do vacation privileges. So the system has to be able to identify each user's location and the benefits for which the person is eligible, and then present a personalized screen for that user.

The technology works well enough that increasing numbers of global firms are implementing worldwide ESS systems to replace all the transactions that used to require a bundle of forms circulating through personnel, benefits, and payroll. Just finding the right forms and processes was time-consuming and irritating for employees; administering the processes was equally so for HR professionals.

But it did help keep the headcount up in HR, and automating transactions like these is one of the reasons HR departments will probably be smaller in the future.

VIRTUAL HR TEAMS

Will e-mail and intranets and video conferencing eliminate the need to meet face to face? Probably not entirely, but companies like Nortel Networks use virtual project teams to plan and implement their global HR policies and procedures. (See "Nortel Networks: Problem Solving Through Virtual Project Teams" in Chapter 7: In Practice.) Steve Kerr, who used to be vice president of leadership development at GE and is now chief learning officer and a managing director at the Goldman Sachs Group, says, "There is no Internet or video conferencing equivalent when you need to bring people together." Then he qualifies that statement.

"One thing I have noticed about the younger generation," he adds, "you put them face-to-face and they can't say five words. But in a chat room they share intimate experiences. Maybe they won't need a whole lot of face-time. Maybe in the future, they will get the same intimacy and sense of sharing that Jack Welch's generation felt had to happen in the meeting room or the golf course."

There's no doubt; there'll be a whole lot of e-changes going on in HR and the rest of the company for some time to come.

E-HR AT NORTEL NETWORKS: POSTER CHILD FOR THE DIGITAL AGE

When you work for an organization that is a leader among companies building the high performance Internet, you should expect to take advantage of cutting-edge technology. At Nortel Networks, the Canada-based telecommunications company that operates in 150 countries, the global HR community indeed does just that.

"We utilize the Web at every opportunity we can – from single items like being able to purchase a *Harvard Business Review* paper online, to being able to deploy people-management tools via the Web to all managers," emphasizes Martin Cozyn, vice president, global compensation and talent strategy.

Thanks to Internet technology, the HR staff can "work at webspeed" with the employee and manager base, he says. They can also research current market practices around the globe from their desktops and use that information to formulate their strategies. Even travel time is more productive now. Travelers use handheld wireless technology to read and reply to e-mail and access the Internet, as well as being accessible by cell phone.

Here are some specific applications of e-technology to HR processes and services at Nortel Networks.

» Employees can securely access their stock options and flexible benefit information via the phone and/or the Web.
» Employees get "one-stop shopping" for all HR-related information on the "Global Web" internal HR Website.
» Employees can recognize their co-workers' outstanding contributions and say "thank you" in real-time by nominating them online for a "PRIDE" award. PRIDE points can then be turned into cash or redeemed for PRIDE catalogue merchandise such as electronics, clothes, jewelry, toys, sporting gear, concierge services or travel, all online.
» HR professionals can access HR-related information on a special Website called "HR Xchange."
» Managers plan all employee salaries, stock options and bonuses using Web-based tools.
» HR professionals everywhere in the world have confidential access to secure HR data and information on all employees electronically. While this has been so for the past 15 years the past few years have brought a convergence of information, so that now HR systems feed into a central data warehouse and link with other non-HR systems. This enables such applications

as sending mass e-mails to specific populations of employees around the world.

» Nortel Networks partnered with Monster.com to create "Job Shop," a groundbreaking Web-based internal career management system.

» An Employee Assistance Program for employees and dependents is available through phone and Web.

» A "Travel Well" service for all employees and their dependents provides online international travel assistance, offering pre-departure health and security information, and expert assistance with health and security emergencies during travel – business or pleasure.

» "Lifeworks" is available to North American employees and their family members at no cost. It is an online resource for expert consultation and information on everyday issues such as house sitting, appliance/home repair, buying big ticket items, health, nutrition, exercise, parenting and child care, legal matters, senior resources, financial issues, disability and accessibility, education and schooling.

» In addition to Websites, the HR community uses chat rooms, Webcasts and e-mail to communicate with managers, employees and HR professionals globally.

NOTES

1 "Global 500 Web Site Recruiting 2001 Survey," Recruitsoft/iLogos Research, available at www.recruitsoft.com.

2 "Best Practices for *Fortune* 500 Career Web Site Recruiting," Recruit-soft/iLogos Research, summary available at www.recruitsoft.com.

3 "Global Recruiting in the Digital Age," SHRM Global Perspectives, SHRM Global Forum, Issue 2 – 2001.

4 "*A Vision of E-Learning for America's Workforce*," (2001) ASTD/ NGA. Downloadable at www.ASTD.com. Other sources offer varying estimates: In *Corporate E-Learning: Exploring a New Frontier*, 2000, WR Hambrecht & Co. (www.wrhambrecht.com) placed the complete technology-based training market for US companies at

$0.47bn in 1999, with Web-based training comprising $0.87bn of that.

5 Gareiss, E. "E-Learning Around the World," *Information Week*, Feb. 26, 2001. www.informationweek.com.

6 "Successful E-Learning Initiatives Abound," *Fortune E-Learning*, www.fortuneelearning.com.

7 Hall, B. & LeCavalier, J. "The Benchmarking Study of Best Practices: E-Learning Across the Enterprise," *E-Learning Magazine*, Sept. 2000. www.elearningmag.com

8 *Corporate E-Learning: Exploring a New Frontier*, 2000, WR Hambrecht & Co. (www.wrhambrecht.com)

The Global Dimension

- » Staffing up with PCNs, HCNs, and TCNs
- » Choosing the right compensation and benefits plans for expats
- » Preparing employees and their families to move abroad – and to return
- » Designing a global performance management system
- » Staying on top of labor laws and customs.

Operating internationally adds layers of complexity to the traditional HR functions of staffing, compensation and benefits, training and development, performance management, and labor relations. This chapter examines each of these, focusing on the additional issues and challenges in organizations that do business around the world. For a discussion of HR's new role as a strategic partner in global enterprises, see Chapter 6: The State of the Art.

STAFFING

To some degree, there's a typical progression in the staffing of international operations. When a company establishes an outpost in another country, it usually sends a management team from the parent country (parent country nationals, or PCNs) on a two-to-three-year assignment to oversee a staff of largely local employees (host country nationals or HCNs). As the local operation matures and the HCNs become savvy in the ways of the organization, PCN presence diminishes until HCNs become the dominant, if not total, management group, reporting to headquarters management, which consists mainly of PCNs in most organizations.

That sequence may be conventional, but it is far from universal. It is affected by a range of factors, which includes the following.

» Host country attitudes and regulations about the hiring and placement of HCNs. A condition of entering the country may be the placement of nationals in key positions right from the start.
» Availability of necessary skills among HCNs. Especially for high tech operations in developing countries, there may not be an available pool of skilled workers to fill even the non-managerial positions. In response, multinational enterprises (MNEs) may look for workers from other countries (third country nationals or TCNs). For example, when Chiyoda Corporation of Japan won a contract to build, own, and operate facilities to exploit and market liquid natural gas in the Emirate of Qatar, there was virtually no available indigenous workforce. To construct the plant, Chiyoda mobilized workers from nearly 40 countries.[1]
» The staffing philosophy of the organization. Some companies prefer to keep PCNs in key positions abroad. That's often called an *ethnocentric* approach. By contrast, other companies may recruit HCN

managers from the start and keep their PCNs at home – a *polycentric* approach.

» Pressures to promote HCN managers into corporate positions. There's a barrier to movement of HCNs into headquarters in both ethnocentric and polycentric organizations. But that barrier too can be broken, creating a two-way flow of nationals – and more work for HR.

» Growing globalization. Finally, there's a growing trend in the most global companies toward a nationality-blind approach to staffing their key positions, both at home and abroad. This approach is called *geocentric*. Making it work requires effective global management development – and/or excellent worldwide head-hunting. So far, there are probably only a handful of companies that truly exemplify this approach. Most of them, like Unilever, Royal Dutch/Shell, and Nestlé, are European in origin.

The decision to staff global operations with PCNs, HCNs, or TCNs often requires balancing the advantages and disadvantages of each.

By using PCNs the organization maintains close control of operations in other countries, assuring compliance with corporate objectives and policies. But PCNs may have trouble adjusting to host country business and social practices, and relying on them is expensive, with studies showing it costs up to four times as much to maintain an employee abroad as it does at home.

Using HCNs helps the company comply with host country requirements or preferences, and build relations in the local business community. It is less costly than relocating PCNs and in the long run helps build a worldwide cadre of talent. But they are likely to be less knowledgeable about company policy and objectives.

TCNs may bring the right technical skills at a lower cost than expatriating PCNs, and if they are from the same region they may have a better understanding than do PCNs of the host country's government, business, and social environments. Using TCNs also contributes to the development of a cadre of international managers, equipped to go anywhere. But in some situations using TCNs may trigger resentment locally, and even touch off deep-seated ethnic or national tensions.

Selecting the right person for the job

Whatever the company philosophy about staffing, there will be international movement in managers, technical experts, and even some administrative staff in an organization that operates in more than one country. Selecting people to make such a move, from either the parent country or a third country, requires weighing a number of criteria.

» *Job-related skills*. It goes without saying you wouldn't send a marine biologist to build a natural gas facility in the desert. Applicable job skills are usually at the top of everyone's list. Unfortunately companies sometimes forget that motivating others and adapting to new surroundings are job skills too.

» *Leadership skills* also rank high on the criteria for placing expatriates. The catch here is that leading people of an entirely different culture sometimes turns out to be a whole new ballgame.

» *Cultural openness and adaptation*. Studies show that more expats cut short their terms abroad because they or their families cannot adapt to the new culture, than because they cannot handle the work they went to do. Yet this may be the most difficult quality to assess in advance, and many companies do only a cursory job of preparing expats and their families for culture shock.

» *Language skills*. MNEs, whatever their parent country, are moving toward adopting English as their corporate language. As a result, language skills rate lower than other needs on most lists of expatriate selection criteria. Nevertheless, an expat who can't converse in the host country language is at a disadvantage in government and local business negotiations, and is almost bound to miss the nuances of employee issues.

» *Willingness to relocate*. For some, international travel spells glamor and excitement, but for many others it threatens family upheaval, isolation from all that is familiar, the interruption of a spouse's career, and even the dislocation of the expat's own. While foreign assignments are often touted as a career advantage, many candidates have seen their colleagues' careers derailed, not boosted, by such a move. These issues are examined further under "Recruiting and Retaining Talent" in Chapter 6: The State of the Art.

HR tasks

With all these staffing variables, it is the responsibility of the HR function to maintain a database of potential candidates for worldwide positions, obtain work permits and entry visas, and provide relocation services ranging from travel to solving housing and schooling problems.

COMPENSATION AND BENEFITS

If staffing internationally sounds complicated, providing compensation and benefits to employees around the world is even more so. Creating compensation plans requires weighing these issues.

» Expatriates need at least to maintain their standard of living in a country where the cost of living, currency, cultural expectations, (e.g. servants), and needs, (e.g. a driver), are not only different, but possibly changing.
» The company's need to incentivize the employee to make the move.
» Parity issues among expatriates and locals, which can be further complicated by the presence of TCNs from a number of countries.
» Solving the problem when expatriates are taxed by both home country and host country authorities.
» What the competition is paying for HCNs in both management and non-management positions and for experienced international managers.

Paying expatriates

Most MNEs compensate expatriates (including TCNs and HCNs on assignment at headquarters) using what is called the *balance sheet approach*. This approach:

» links expatriates' base pay to their home country salary level;
» provides an additional incentive as an inducement to make the move;
» provides allowances to cover additional expenditures – cost of living, housing, etc.;
» makes allowances for double taxation, usually by paying host country taxes for the employee; and
» usually provides for a portion of the base pay to be in local currency and a portion in home country currency, modifying the impact of currency fluctuations (on both company and employee).

While the balance sheet approach works to maintain expatriates' standard of living and equity with their colleagues back home, it can create unsettling disparities between expatriates and host country nationals, and among expatriates from several countries working together in a host country. And it requires the company to regularly update its cost-of-living data for countries around the world, and adjust compensation accordingly.

Other approaches

While it is not as popular as the balance sheet approach, there is another approach to compensating expatriates that has adherents among some MNEs. It is sometimes called the *going rate approach*[2], and its key feature is that it links base salary to the going rate in the host country, not the home country. Obviously it is popular with expatriates moving into countries where salaries are high, and less popular for moves into low-paying countries. So, if salaries in the host country are low, the company may sweeten the package with supplements. The advantage is parity between host country nationals and expatriates, but there may be glaring differences between the pay for the same job in different countries.

One criticism of the dominant balance sheet approach is that, by including allowances for so many variables, it forces the company into a role that intrudes on the employee's private life. In response to that and to simplify administration, some companies are trying a *lump sum approach*[3] to compensation. Instead of paying separate allowances for each variable, the company pays its relocating employee one lump sum to cover all added expenses, and lets the employee choose how to spend it. This approach is relatively easy to administer and non-intrusive, but it does provide a risk for employees whose skills for managing money are not well developed.

Whatever approach an MNE takes to compensation it is often just the beginning of the total pay package, which probably includes bonuses, incentive plans, and possibly stock options or other forms of employee ownership plans. Stock options plans are most popular among US-based multinationals, with some European companies such as Royal Dutch/Shell following suit. But stock option plans have international limitations; there are taxation and regulatory issues to deal with in each country. Planning and administering all these pay components is complicated by worldwide differences in expectations, practices, and regulations.

Benefits

The benefits manager of an MNE confronts a mind-boggling array of government programs and standard practices, and is faced with assimilating them all into some semblance of parity for employees around the world and ensuring that travel won't cause an employee to lose accrued benefits, such as pensions. In the Unites States, health insurance is at the top of everyone's benefits list, but in most countries, health care is provided by a tax-supported system. Many countries have mandated vacation times, and in virtually all countries except the United States, Japan, Canada, and Mexico, four weeks or more of vacation is standard even if it's not regulated.

Companies may have to decide whether to maintain expatriates in their home country social security system or to enroll them in host country ones. For perpetual TCNs this can be a real issue, since they may never have been in one country long enough to accrue significant coverage.

In the past, studies have indicated that multinationals have done a good job of providing for the retirement needs of their PCNs, but less so for TCNs. New approaches will be influenced not only by the needs of new cadres of international managers, but also by the movement away from traditional pension plans to more portable ones and by the decreased expectation that employees will stay with one firm until retirement.

TRAINING AND DEVELOPMENT

Training and development programs geared to global issues fall into two categories: pre-departure training and job-related training.

The best pre-departure programs include site visits by the candidate for relocation and spouse (or partner); orientation to the country and the culture for both employee and partner; job orientation; language training; counseling on compensation, benefits, taxes, housing and other location-specific issues; and counseling by repatriates. Although it is much less common, preparation for repatriation as an assignment draws to a close is important too. Repatriates need career counseling, since it's not at all unusual for them to return to a company that has restructured and held no spot open for them. And after a couple of years abroad, they and their families can benefit from reorientation to their home culture.

But broader issues of training and development lie in preparing people for leadership roles in international operations.

"For everyone in business, probably the most urgent challenge is developing leaders," states Warren Wilhelm, an expert in leadership development, organization development, and human resource management. He is president of the Global Consulting Alliance and also teaches at the Thunderbird School in Glendale, Arizona. Global companies, he adds, have the additional complication of needing people who can lead in different cultures. The learning challenge is to help leaders learn how to be more effective and to do it quickly. Developing as a leader, Wilhelm asserts, "takes a combination of learning factual knowledge and experiencing enough challenge so that one is constantly learning from day-to-day activities."

An effective leadership development program may have several components, including the following.

» *A variety of developmental job experiences.* In global companies, those experiences can be all over the world. Picking the right jobs, advises Wilhelm, requires identifying what the potential leader needs to learn, then finding a job that will challenge the person in that area. "Leave your potential leaders in these jobs just long enough to learn about 80% of what the job needs," he recommends. "Then move them on just before they are ready."
» *Coaching.* This goes hand in hand with changing job assignments. It's important whether the skills that need developing are technical or interpersonal ones. Potential learners may need factual knowledge or they may need to learn how to analyze data and draw conclusions from it. They may need to improve their ability to communicate or develop better interpersonal relationships with people like suppliers, customers, or co-workers. They may, suggests Wilhelm, need to develop better bearing or presence. And when they are traveling from country to country they need to learn to be culturally adept, able to operate effectively within various cultures.

» *Classroom experiences*. Following the lead of GE's famous Croton-ville education center, some MNEs have their own "universities" where rising stars from throughout the world come together for total immersion into corporate culture, corporate values, and corporate strategies, and to build their own skills for applying what they learn back on the job while honoring local culture and business practices. MNEs also send people to international business schools for either degree programs or executive development programs. (See "Developing Global Leaders" in Chapter 6: The State of the Art, for more on leadership development.)

PERFORMANCE MANAGEMENT

Managing the performance of employees through the annual or semi-annual cycle of goal-setting, monitoring and feedback, and performance appraisal poses some added difficulties when those employees are spread around the world. From the beginning of the cycle to the end, such issues as the following can arise that complicate the process.

» Conflicts between the strategic goals of the MNE and the goals of the host country. How does the local manager respond to both?
» Goals set by headquarters that, in the view of the local manager, fail to take into account local conditions. These can range from financial goals that are at odds with local accounting systems, to performance goals that ignore host country business practices and regulations.
» Physical separation that limits ongoing discourse and feedback for locals who report to headquarters managers far away. Thousands of words by telephone and e-mail can't always take the place of first-hand observance.
» Deciding who does the appraisals: the boss at headquarters whose contact is limited? Or should the company use 360-degree appraisals seeking input from locals as well, and perhaps even customers?
» Cultural differences between headquarters and local personnel. This is especially an issue for HCNs who may not be conditioned to the appraisal process used by the MNE. For example, the western practice of tackling performance problems head-on may prove coun-terproductive in cultures where avoiding direct confrontation is the norm.

Despite the difficulties – in fact, because of the difficulties – performance management may be even more important among global operations than in domestic ones, where all too often it gets more lip service than participation. Working through the performance management process forces the organization to confront and overcome obstacles that, if ignored, could cause unit-wide performance problems rather than individual ones.

LABOR RELATIONS

Because labor relations practices vary greatly among countries, most MNEs leave responsibility for managing this function to the local HR managers. Even an adamantly union-free company probably has to relax its stance if it wants to operate in many countries. Still, labor relations is far too important for headquarters to ignore, so corporate HR may monitor or provide oversight for local labor negotiations.

While it may not be possible for a central HR function to know the intricacies of labor law and practices in every country where a giant MNE operates, it is important to keep track of a number of issues for each location.

» To what extent does the government regulate the employer-labor relationship?
» Does the location fall under directives from some other body such as the Organization for Economic Co-operation and Development, or the European Union?
» Are labor negotiations conducted at the union-employer level, or between industry-wide unions and employers' associations?
» Are unions guaranteed joint decision-making power with management through a seat on the board of directors, or through works councils that share power with operations management?
» Can competing unions operate within the same shop?
» Are managers unionized?
» Is it possible to operate union free?
» Do unions have strong political or religious affiliations?
» Even if union membership is low in terms of numbers, is union power still something to contend with?
» What topics are usually covered in labor contracts?

» Must all employees belong to the union, i.e. is it a closed shop?
» What are the government regulations regarding discipline, grievances, and terminations? Are there regulatory obstacles to terminating employees or closing a facility? Is compensation required even for employees terminated for cause?
» How forcefully can and would labor fight any move to a location with lower labor costs, e.g. to Mexico from its northern NAFTA partners or, within the European Union, from a northern country to Portugal?

Starting from the premise that it is labor's task to keep wages up and jobs at home, and it is the MNE's task to locate where labor costs – relative to quality – are lowest, there is a potential for perpetual tension. It's the responsibility of MNEs to keep that tension at a productive rather than disruptive level.

BEST PRACTICES FOR PERFORMING HR FUNCTIONS IN A GLOBAL ENVIRONMENT

» Take a nationality-blind approach to staffing for local and headquarters operations.
» Ensure that, when their assignments are over, expatriates have jobs to move into that take advantage of their experience and new skills.
» Develop compensation policies for expatriates that both provide an incentive for going abroad, and are perceived as fair by parent country and host country counterparts. In the age of the Internet you can't keep salaries a secret.
» Pay particular attention to benefits for third country nationals who spend their careers moving around from country to country. They may fall through both home country and host country security nets.
» Provide both pre-departure training and repatriation training to ease the culture shock both ways.
» Ensure that outcome-based performance management programs are based on goals that match local and corporate needs.
» Stay on top of key labor laws and practices in all host countries.

NOTES

1 Ishikura, M., Kadoyama, A., & Kikkawa, Y. "1999 International Project of the Year: Qatargas LNG Plant Project," *PM Network*, January 2000.

2 Dowling, P.J., Welch, D.E., & Schuler, R.S. (1999) *International Human Resource Management: Managing People in a Multinational Context*. South-Western, Cincinnati, OH.

3 Briscoe, D.R. (1995) *International Human Resource Management*. Prentice Hall, Paramus, NJ.

The State of the Art

» Recruiting and retaining the best talent
» Developing global leaders
» Proving HR's value as a strategic business partner
» Forecasting HR's future.

If you can't put it online, outsource it. Better yet, outsource it and let the vendor put it online. Those are the messages that are shaking up the HR community, whether domestic or global. Many companies are outsourcing their payroll function, benefits administration, information systems and record keeping, pension plan administration, and a host of other activities that are long on data entry and short on decision making. Of course, they've been going to vendors for training for years. The tasks that still have to be done in-house – like filling out forms – can often be done online directly by the employee without having to pass through the hands of an HR administrator.

That said, nobody's suggesting that HR should just go away – although *Fortune* magazine writer Thomas A. Stewart did use words like "Deep-six it ... turn it into road kill."[1] But in a follow-up article, he pointed out that he had called his recommendation "a modest proposal." So unless we believe that the literary icon Jonathan Swift was really making a case for cannibalism in his *A Modest Proposal*, we should accept Stewart's explanation that he was "facetiously advocating something outrageous to provoke a discussion of something serious."[2]

Certainly there has been a flurry of discussion about the proper role of HR, most of it advocating that it should become sleek, focused, and strategic; that it should be, as author, teacher, and consultant Dave Ulrich predicts, a lot smaller with a lot more impact. In the global arena HR innovators are maximizing their impact by concentrating on:

» recruiting and retaining the best talent;
» developing global leaders; and
» proving their value as strategic business partners.

This chapter will discuss these things and examine the capabilities HR professionals need to master their new roles.

RECRUITING AND RETAINING TALENT

Searching outside

The cry for new talent had reached a wail before the economy took a downturn in 2000. If the next set of surveys shows that recruiting and retaining good people has been bounced from the top of the key issues list for global HR, that will be unfortunate. A floundering economy

THE STATE OF THE ART

makes it easier to find bodies; the job list is shorter and the job seeker list is longer. But it doesn't diminish the need to attract and retain the *best* people. That belongs on the key issues list in good times and bad because the companies that can do it have the best chance to survive and prosper in any economy.

If outsourcing is such a great idea, why should HR be in the recruiting business, you might ask. Why not turn it over to a professional recruitment firm? Indeed, the task of shaking out good external candidates is often done more efficiently by outside recruiters; and certainly line managers, not HR people, make the final choices for all but the lowliest jobs. But HR has a crucial role to play in defining job requirements and critical capabilities. David Ulrich maintains that it is HR's responsibility to help the company define the capabilities it needs to fulfill its strategy. After that, HR can start looking for the right people, outside and in, to support those company capabilities.

Looking for the right new people to support global capabilities often takes companies to colleges and universities outside of their parent country borders. Global companies compete for graduates of the top international business schools, such as the International Institute for Management Development (IMD) in Lausanne, Switzerland; INSEAD in Fontainebleau, France; the London Business School; or the Thunderbird School in Glendale, Arizona, where half the students are from outside the United States.

Once they have defined the capabilities they need for success, companies also look for new hires in some nontraditional places. After it identified a need for collaborative people who would focus on service and be at home in its worldwide network of operations, one of the places in which GE began to recruit was the Indian Institute of Technology.

Recruiting within

For every job that a company hires an outsider for, there are plenty of others that get filled from within. Unfortunately, it is still not common for corporate HR in multinational enterprises to keep track of high-potential managers coming up through the ranks in subsidiaries. That's partly because many companies are still operating around the world from an ethnocentric mindset, barely considering their host country nationals as a potential talent pool for top positions. It's also because the HR people themselves often lack overseas experience and a truly global mindset.

The trendsetters, like Unilever and IBM, are developing global databases, tracking promising managers throughout the world.[3] IBM made its database of senior managers worldwide over a decade ago and is building a much broader one of worldwide employees. Unilever has talent pools that include individual companies, foreign subsidiaries, and corporate headquarters. They use these to identify an international cadre they can tap into to find the right person with the right skills to move into headquarters or third country positions, regardless of national origin.

Such databases include items like experiences, technical and business skills, language skills, interests, and developmental activities (experienced and planned). In some companies inclusion is voluntary, and keeping the database updated is the responsibility of participating individuals (probably nudged by HR). But the most important thing is that these companies *use* the databases, both for filling jobs and for planning training. People will keep their own information up to date when they know the company searches the database to make job assignments. They'll ignore it fast if the company ignores it too.

The other half of the match-up between talent and jobs is a complete description of the capabilities required for each position – and not just the technical or business skills. To succeed in top management requires leadership skills, and to succeed in international positions requires cultural flexibility, interpersonal skills for dealing with people whose perspective and expectations differ from one's own, and tolerance – or better, enthusiasm – for the unknown, the unexpected, and sometimes the uncontrollable. HR needs to find out, not assume, what specific capabilities are required for each job.

It's equally important to know who, among the potential talent pool, is willing to relocate across borders. If willingness is an obstacle, it may be because of two issues that are getting a lot of attention these days.

» *The dual-career conflict.* The days of the supportive, loyal trailing spouse are long passed. Many high potential employees are married to people with challenging and ambitious careers of their own. And those spouses don't leap at the chance to exchange their income and their spot on their own advancement ladder for an opportunity to keep house in a foreign country for a couple of years.

It's a problem with no easy answers. MNEs are trying a number of inducements, from cash to career help. Royal Dutch/Shell provides both – and more. The cash, up to $8,000, is money the spouse can use to take courses, go to conferences, get certifications, or fund any career development activities. The career help is primarily through the Shell Spouse Employment Network, a support group that operates worldwide with Web connectivity and offers support, coaching, and counseling. It is staffed by Shell employees.

But in some countries the problem is bigger than just finding a job. Some countries, like the United States, do not give work permits to spouses of expatriates. So trailing spouses entering the United States can't work unless they stay long enough to obtain a green card (the commonly used term for an Alien Registration Card, which is actually pink). Shell is a founding member of a coalition of 20 companies called Permits, a lobby group working to change work permit policies around the world. Working with US-based organizations, Mews and LPA (Labor Policy Association), the coalition is focusing on the US, where a bill in Congress proposes relaxing work permit restrictions for working spouses of expatriate employees.

» *The out-of-sight, out-of-mind syndrome.* In a number of companies operating internationally, people return home from overseas assignments shocked to discover that, not only is there no corner office awaiting them, there's barely a workspace at all. Instead of being that career-boosting experience they were promised, their time abroad left them out of the loop when promotions or reorganizations occurred. Now they are back, and nobody knows what to do with them or seems to believe that their experiences abroad are in any way applicable to what's happening at home.

That corporate attitude derails careers and motivates an unexpectedly high exit rate among repatriates. It also discourages others from packing their bags to go abroad. Any up-and-comer with open eyes only has to see that happen to a couple of colleagues to say "Uh-uh," when an offer to relocate comes around.

But it is a situation that can be changed. Companies that make an effort to retain and reward people with international experience set an example that encourages other employees to take international assignments. These companies think repatriation from the time the new expatriate departs. Some enterprises provide expatriates with mentors to keep them up to date about organizational changes and to keep reminding the home organization that the expatriate exists and is developing important skills. They also do career planning that is always looking one or two jobs ahead. And they value international experience and take advantage of it when the person returns.

DEVELOPING GLOBAL LEADERS

"The more unlike the present is the future, the more you need leadership," says Steve Kerr, chief learning officer and a managing director at the Goldman Sachs Group. Former chief learning officer and vice president of leadership development at General Electric, Kerr is one of the world's most respected experts in the field of leadership development.

The faster change of pace in today's world is one of the reasons why Kerr thinks developing leaders is more important now than it ever was. Another reason is that the value of other resources has declined. He gives a couple of examples: "In the United States and some other countries, patent protection is getting weaker. And the Internet has reduced barriers to entry. If you want to sell cars, you open up a Website and you are selling an hour later." So the ability to get more work out of people ends up being the last sustainable competitive advantage.

Drawing from his experience at GE and Goldman Sachs, Kerr provides a model for leadership development:

1 *"If you don't have a target, you can't judge the flight of every arrow."*

First, create a template of the attributes you want, based on what you believe in as an organization. That requires a reassessment of organizational needs and values. Kerr uses GE examples to explain: "In the old days, GE made a lot of money around turbines and engines. Now it's more like give them the shaver and sell them the blades. You make your money on spares and services. That tells you what determines success: people who are collaborative and sell service, not the big game hunters."

Identifying your target informs your recruiting, training, and measurements.

2 *"Ability × motivation = performance. You've got to make them want to change."*

Part of motivating people is rewarding the right things. Goldman Sachs, Kerr maintains, has always been different from the typical Wall Street firm, being team-oriented rather than nurturing superstars. Goldman Sachs recruits for team players, not glory hounds. And yet, he admits, that mindset doesn't quite match the reward system. "Somehow," he says, "the big rewards go to the commercially successful person." That's probably because teamwork is harder to measure than results. So part of his job is to develop a measurement system so Goldman Sachs can better reward the qualities it values.

Another aspect of motivating people is helping them understand how their job fits in and contributes to the success of the company – what Kerr calls the "line of sight." People have to know what, in their day-to-day jobs, each of them can do to help the company.

3 *"Train on the things that matter."*

Kerr illustrates with another GE example: "In the old days at Crotonville, they had a game called Win as Much as You Can. When we wanted to emphasize teamwork we took that out and put in different games around win-win."

Training on the things that matter also means giving people the training or other developmental experience that matters to them at a particular point in time. Kerr calls it education built to order instead of education built to inventory. One way to do that is to tie leadership development to transitions. So, for people with no direct reports but who need to get work done through others, GE offers a course on influence without authority. "Later when they have people to manage you teach them about hierarchical systems," he adds.

People in international assignments have more transitions, so they need more developmental experiences. "Maybe you are being asked to manage a workforce in a place where you don't speak the language. Or maybe you manage across time zones. Those changes lead to more developmental experiences."

4 *"Never send a trained person back to an untrained environment."*

It's a familiar scenario. Someone goes off to an intensive offsite training and development experience and gets revved up to go back to the job and make changes. What greets the person upon return, however, is a desk full of stuff and a boss who is indifferent to the trainee's new "religion." It doesn't take long before the energy and enthusiasm fade and life goes back to what passes for normal.

Kerr's solution: don't bring individuals into training; bring in teams – teams with a project and with a boss back home who is committed to the process. At GE, teams from the leadership development programs presented their learnings and recommendations for action to the company's top 30 people. Many of these recommendations have made a big difference in GE. One, for example, resulted in building staff in South America.

At Goldman Sachs, participants in the company's two-day program for all managers have gone before the company's management committee and presented two items. The first item is what they learned that they can and will implement on their own. The second item is something they learned that would help Goldman Sachs but that they can't do alone. For that they request permission and support.

Leadership development only works when the organization is committed to supporting change.

5 *"If you know you are being measured on how much you change, you go back determined to change."*

To measure changes in leadership that result from training, Kerr says to start by describing the behaviors that are likely to change if the course is successful. Prior to training, show those descriptions of behavior to four or five people who know each participant. Ask, how often do you see the person doing this now? A few months after training, go back to the assessors and ask them the same question. "I know it's impossible to prove cause and effect," Kerr says, to mollify the critics who maintain you can't measure training because there are too many other variables that also affect behavior, "but if people change in the direction of the course, I'm happy to take credit."

(There's more about Kerr's take on global leadership in the section on "Key Thinkers" in Chapter 8: Key Concepts and Thinkers.)

International experience

One thing all the experts agree is crucial for developing global leaders is ensuring they get international experience. Royal Dutch/Shell Group of Companies has 6,000 expatriates in its workforce, probably the most of any company in the world. All of Shell's top 50 executives have lived a significant part of their lives outside their home countries. All new management recruits take an overseas assignment in their first five years. And Shell people know it will give their careers a boost if they accept a job in a difficult location.

Unilever, another company in the rarified ranks of truly global, recruits graduates of universities in the countries where it operates – then often sends them somewhere else in the course of their careers. Nigel Hurst, senior vice president of HR for Home and Personal Care North America, draws a vivid international picture: "So we've got Indonesians in Australia, Brits in the US, Australians in China. We try to build up a strong local understanding of the countries where we operate – about 87- along with an international mindset." As well as sending people on extended work assignments abroad, Unilever also sends managers on "secondments," or short-term assignments of six, nine, or twelve months. This is one way for fairly new managers to have an international experience. Often their task is to travel abroad to find out how something is done in a particular location, then return and apply what they've learned at home.

HR AS STRATEGIC BUSINESS PARTNER

In a recent survey of HR leaders in 50 top global companies by the Society for Human Resource Management (SHRM) Global Forum, nearly all of the respondents said they were involved in strategic decision-making.[4] That involvement often takes the form of participation in the company's strategy team.

The Royal Dutch/Shell Group of Companies has had such a team for the past four years. John Hofmeister, group HR director, describes how it operates:

> "At Shell we have a strategy team: the five managing directors, the head of strategy, the head of finance, and the head of HR, as well as the CEOs of the major businesses – about 12 or 13 people.

We spend time throughout the year looking forward to long-term strategy as well as looking at the next couple of years' strategy. We all have a place at the table. We're all expected to take a view on the external market drivers and the external social and political realities. We're all expected to be well-read, well versed in what's going on in the world, and to express our views about strategic direction. Every business has a principal on its strategy. We're all expected to comment on each principal's view of strategy.''

Not only does the team look at each business' strategy, but, as Hofmeister explains,

"We think beyond the businesses to the white spaces between the businesses, and we ask ourselves, 'What do we need to do to make sure that the strategic spectrum is covered, not just strategic silos, so the white space can result in other business?' ''

Besides participating in the business strategy process, as head of HR he has another strategic role:

"Clearly when it comes to strategy, I do have a particular responsibility for the HR side of it. We have a Shell Group strategy; then every business has its strategy; then we have a people strategy that enables the business strategies. So we're talking about three different dimensions here. Shell's people strategy is very much dependent upon developing affiliations between people and Shell. A lot of companies are treating people like, 'When you need 'em, you need 'em, and when you don't, you don't.' We've developed a strategy around a priority of affiliation.''

(For details of Shell's HR strategy, see "Royal Dutch/ Shell's Global HR Strategy" in Chapter 7: In Practice.)

WHAT'S AHEAD FOR GLOBAL HR?

One of the biggest changes in HR's future is one that will affect both global and domestic companies. Remember how this chapter started: if you can't put it online, outsource it. That trend is going to change the face and the impact of HR.

As Dave Ulrich explains, HR is increasingly being split into two parts. The first part he calls "transaction work: things like payroll, benefits, hiring, registration for training." He has identified three phases in the movement of transaction work out of in-house HR departments. First, companies created regional service centers with 800 numbers to respond to employees' needs and questions. Currently, many companies are very aggressively putting these functions online, so employees can access them and handle their own transactions at any time. Typically, as companies do that, they disband the regional service centers and centralize the maintenance of the online function. Finally, he predicts, these centers will be increasingly outsourced so companies will no longer even be maintaining these intranet sites. Companies like BP and Bank of America, he points out, have already outsourced their online HR transaction work. He notes one global firm with 1500 HR employees that expects to reduce the department's size to 600 within five years.[5]

When you split off the transaction work, you are left with a much smaller-sized HR department doing the second part: what Ulrich calls translation work. That work, he affirms, will not be outsourced. It's work that is much more central to business and has much more impact. At its heart, this work involves organizational diagnosis. It requires assessing the capabilities necessary to succeed based upon the organization's current strategies, and then building an organization with those capabilities.

Ulrich has identified four roles for HR professionals in this compact new HR environment: coaches for business leaders, providing performance feedback; organizational architects, drawing up plans for action; builders who deliver the HR practices for implementing strategy; and facilitators of teams to manage change.

There's one more thing that will be expected of HR leaders, Ulrich adds – and it's a very big responsibility – to serve as the conscience of the organization, modeling the value-set that enables the company to be successful.

More challenges for HR professionals

Vladimir Pucik, professor of international human resources at the International Institute for Management Development (IMD) at Lausanne, Switzerland, adds two additional challenges for HR professionals in the next few years.

» To define what they do in terms of creating value for external customers. "HR people have often said they have only internal customers," he declares. "That's dangerous. The accountants call those people overhead. A focus solely on satisfying internal customers leads easily to a bits-and-pieces approach to human resources management, rather than to one that is internally consistent and externally coherent. The bits and the pieces can easily be outsourced since there is typically someone who can do these separate activities cheaper and better."

So how does HR create value for external customers? First, talk to the external customers. Second, make sure that the organization acts to meet current and future external customer needs. HR contributes to that by, among other things, the kind of people they hire, train, and retain, and by identifying the behaviors to be encouraged and rewarded, Pucik says.

» To differentiate themselves from their competitors. That's a big issue for HR, he says, because historically HR worldwide is built not on differentiation, but rather on benchmarking. "If you don't want to be different, how can you create competitive advantage?" he asks. HR has to be willing to take more risks in promoting unique organizational solutions, he maintains. "Nobody can win a Formula One race by building an average car." This also implies that the key HR role is to focus on organizational performance. Without this, there is no need for HR; custodial administration is all that a company would require.

Finally, there's another dimension where Pucik would like to see HR become more active: the social dimension. He refers to Royal Dutch/Shell's *Shell Report* to illustrate. In it, Shell talks about the social impact of its operations around the world.

Pucik explains, "On the one hand we talk about achievements of the market economy, and at the same time, we acknowledge that the market economy creates certain contradictions and tensions in the world. You get winners and losers." He adds, "I don't see HR providing a solution, but at least I'd like to see it generating debate and developing leaders that understand the issues."

NOTES

1 Stewart, T.A. "Taking on the Last Bureaucracy," *Fortune*, Jan. 1, 1996.

2 Stewart, T.A. "Human Resources Bites Back," *Fortune*, June 13, 1996.

3 Quelch, J.A. & Bloom, H. "Ten Steps to a Global Human Resources Strategy", *Strategy + Business*, 1st Quarter, 1999. Available online at www.sblogin.com.

4 Reported on www.shrmglobal.org/publications/hrworld/leaders. htm.

5 Ulrich, D. (2001) "HR Audit," working paper, August.

In Practice

» HR the high-tech way
» HR management from a subsidiary's viewpoint
» An HR strategy to support high growth.

This chapter zeros in on three companies, each with vast international operations and each with different strengths in its HR. The first study tells how Nortel Networks used an international project team to tackle a talent retention issue. The second looks at Matsushita's hands-off approach to HR in its overseas operations from the point of view of the head of HR in its North American subsidiary. In the third, the head of global HR at Royal Dutch/Shell describes the company's HR strategy, providing insights into what is important now in the company that most people agree is one of the world's most global organizations.

NORTEL NETWORKS: PROBLEM SOLVING THROUGH VIRTUAL PROJECT TEAMS

Telecommunications giant Nortel Networks, which has corporate head-quarters in Canada and operates in 150 countries, calls its people management strategy "Talent Leadership." Its goal, says Martin Cozyn, vice president, global compensation and talent strategy, (in a response to the author's questionnaire) is "to create a high-performance Internet culture that reflects the diverse workforce demands and demographics of a global Internet economy, and maximizes individual contribution, organizational performance and profitability."

Achieving that goal requires retaining top talent, and Nortel Networks was beginning to identify a problem there. It was also apparent why the problem was occurring. What was happening was that managers tended to treat everybody pretty much the same when it came to allocating rewards. They clustered everyone around the midpoint, reluctant to give any really high or very low awards.

Predictably, that resulted in some unhappy high performers when they realized that others who contributed much less were being rewarded pretty much the same as they were. Too often they left the company, lured by new employers who were ready to recognize the difference they made. Meanwhile the lower contributors were motivated to stay. One point in the Nortel Networks global HR strategy took direct aim at this problem.

» Creating a high-performance culture that continuously identifies and differentiates outstanding contributors by rewarding them with financial rewards and development opportunities proportional to their individual contribution.

Other elements in the strategy supported that intent.

» Staying on the pulse of what's important to employees (through direct feedback using Web technology, surveys, focus groups and one-on-one open dialogues), and on what the competition is offering.
» Basing competitive compensation and rewards packages on what employees say they value, including financial rewards, development opportunities and work/life flexibility.
» Paying for individual value and skill set, not entitlement and hierarchy.
» Aggressively open and honest communications to keep employees engaged, solicit real-time feedback, answer questions and communicate business priorities and successes.

Having acknowledged they had work to do, the members of the Nortel Networks global HR community set out to tackle the issue in the way they work best – through an international integrated project team.

"When we design any global program we have a network of individuals that we 'tap' into to represent the regional view," Cozyn explains. "These individuals form an integrated project team with a team leader/project manager, and have specific deliverables and outcomes they are responsible for. The project team may be short-term – together long enough to develop the strategy – or may be longer-term to also prime the deployment of the program."

Pulling together such a team requires close co-operation among the key groups within HR at Nortel Networks: *Strategy HR*, which examines the market issues, interprets the Nortel Networks business strategy and sets the Talent Leadership agenda; *Business HR*, which develops the appropriate "Talent Agenda" for each Nortel Networks business, in line with the global HR strategy; and *Services HR*, which designs and delivers HR processes and programs to managers and employees globally.

Strategy HR identified the need for a "Talent Segmentation" process that would differentiate talent based on each person's relative level of contribution. Designing, developing, and implementing a program to do that began with tapping one person to be project manager: Shelagh Best, who had worked on many strategic HR project teams to develop tools and processes, including the Nortel Networks performance management tool, Priorities, and helped shape the philosophy behind Talent Leadership. Best was accountable for driving, designing, and implementing the Talent Segmentation process for all of Nortel Networks.

But she was far from alone. Working with her was a project team of HR professionals pulled together from all three of the company's major regions – the Americas (including Brazil and Latin America), EMEA (Europe, Middle East and Africa), and Asia-Pacific. The team's task was to develop the global strategy, process and tools for Talent Segmentation.

Working for one of the world's leading providers of Internet and telecommunications technology, Nortel Networks people are used to virtual environments, perfectly comfortable working on teams where communication is much more likely to be via technology than face-to-face. That allows real-time connections among far-flung members with a minimum of airplane travel. This team was no exception. To collaborate and share information 24/7, they had at their disposal:

» secure servers;
» private intranet (which, by the way, encompasses 5.9-million Web pages, not that the team needed to access them all);
» audio conferencing;
» video conferencing;
» Meeting Manager (a Web-based presentation tool that allows users to present or view slides in sync with other attendees of multi-site meetings); and
» NetMeeting (Microsoft's real-time collaboration tool for meetings or individuals working together. It allows for text "chat sessions," file transfers, graphic whiteboard to share real-time diagrams/visuals, video and audio conferencing.)

Thanks to technology, the globally-dispersed team members could work closely with each other, but they didn't operate in a virtual ivory tower. As their direction and process evolved, they continuously consulted with their business contacts in each of the regions and with other key groups such as Business Ethics and Compliance, Employee Relations, and Legal to validate the direction and solicit input.

Through this process Best and the team developed an overarching strategy and philosophy, which it expressed as the need to continually identify and motivate the top contributors of the company, to create a high-performance culture that rewards outstanding contributions.

After getting buy-in from the business leaders, the team tackled its next step, implementation. It divided into smaller sub-teams, each focused on a specific task such as tool development, communication, and information services integration. The sub-teams leveraged the help of the business and regional HR teams as well as the Global Program Office, which is part of the Services HR organization and acts as the global "data depot."

The sub-teams developed tools to help managers understand Talent Segmentation philosophy and conduct reviews, including the "Talent Segmentation Support Tool;" an Excel spreadsheet that provides a common business standard to assess individual contributions; a worksheet to assist managers in assessing the value-add their employees bring to the business; and a planning guide to help managers take action after completing the reviews. A communications sub-team also developed a guidebook with frequently asked questions and answers, and a memo template that could be customized and sent from each business leader. With the program underway, the project team disbanded, transitioning the operation of Talent Segmentation to the Global Program Office team, which is responsible for updating the data with each round of Talent Segmentation, and ensuring ongoing data integrity.

The program also has a "program owner" – Mary-Michelle Brown, who is part of Strategy HR, and whose job is to continually measure the program's success, evaluate the philosophy in line with business strategy, and initiate changes as appropriate to ensure it stays current.

The Talent Segmentation philosophy is also applied to other areas, Cozyn adds. "Employee compensation is now determined by both the market value of people's skills and their level of contribution or talent segment. For example, when we paid out our six-month bonus for the second half of 2000, we ensured that employees were paid according to their contributions. This was applied worldwide and was effective because the global HR team was involved in the design and implementation as were the global management team. Attrition is also measured using segmentation principles."

The outcome

Thanks to Talent Segmentation, Nortel Networks now has a process that can be used to carry out these crucial HR functions.

» To retain top talent – understand who they are, talk to them about what they want from their experience at Nortel Networks, and put in place individual compensation, development, and career strategies that reflect their interests and aspirations.
» To put top performers in roles where they will have the greatest impact.
» To build high performing teams that will get the company to market first with solutions customers value, and upgrade leadership bench strength for future growth opportunities.
» To focus management attention on the lowest contributors so that they will be dealt with appropriately; either helped to improve or weeded out.

LESSONS FROM NORTEL NETWORKS

The Nortel Networks approach to retaining and motivating employees offers several insights for other global HR organizations, particularly those that are well networked.

» Recognize when taking the easy way out on touchy issues becomes a norm, and take action. Talent Segmentation tackled an issue that is pervasive in many organizations. It's easier for managers to rate everyone the same than to differentiate between adequate and exceptional, or – even harder – to confront poor performers. More companies need to take the Nortel Networks route and change the norm.
» Enlist people from around the world to tackle a problem together. Cozyn claims that "At Nortel Networks we don't separate 'corporate HR' from 'local HR' the way traditional companies do. Our entire corporate HR function is global, of which local teams are an important component."
» Don't work in an isolated HR enclave. Enlist the co-operation and input of business units and other support functions.

> » Use communications technology to its fullest. With the latest voice and data communication advances, there's no reason for people to be separated by geography.
> » Use teams to solve problems, but make sure there's an individual who's accountable for results.

MATSUSHITA: WHEN IN THE US ...

Matsushita Electric Industrial Company (MEI) of Japan, manufacturers of Panasonic and other consumer and industrial brands, takes an approach to worldwide human resources management that is 180 degrees different from that of Nortel Networks. Which just goes to show there is more than one way to run a multinational enterprise.

While Nortel Networks takes a globally integrated approach, emphasizing that, "At Nortel Networks, we don't separate 'corporate HR' from 'local HR,' " MEI makes a definite distinction. Around the world, Matsushita operations develop their own HR policies in accordance with the laws and customs of the host country.

In an interview Bill Schupp, vice president of North American personnel for Matsushita Electric Corporation of America described the HR operation in the US pretty simply: "We're set up like any other company in the United States." To him, that just makes sense since the laws, customs, and expectations are so different from those in Japan.

He gave the author some examples. "Compensation and benefits are very different. In Japan MEI owns its own hospitals. It provides medical care, not medical insurance. The compensation system in Japan is based partly on position, partly on age, number of dependents, the age of children, and very little on performance. A person who is married with three children makes more than a single person in the same job." That's a far cry from the US subsidiary's variable pay system with bonuses based on completion of objectives.

He describes his relationship with the head of HR in Japan as, "I give him some reports." These reports cover HR trends and developments in North American business, identify which of these might be implemented in Matsushita's North American operations, and analyze their potential impact on Matsushita's business. But there are no HR policies, nor even broad-brush guidelines that come from Japan.

That doesn't mean there is no exchange of information between HR in the parent company and in the US subsidiary. Recently, the Japanese head of HR has been asking Schupp about performance management and 401k plans – popular, employer-sponsored retirement plans that allow employees to contribute part of their salaries, with contributions often partly matched by the employer. All contributions and earnings are tax-deferred until withdrawal. Following the lead of its US subsidiary, the Japanese parent is working on implementing these, even looking at making compensation a variable by performance.

There are, of course, differences between managing HR in a purely domestic company and managing HR in a company owned by a foreign parent. For one thing, while it is common these days for western companies to have company values posted on their walls or enclosed in acrylic paperweights, it is not common for those values to have been penned by a Japanese businessman in the 1930s. Matsushita's *Basic Business Principles* were written by the company founder, Konosuke Matsushita (usually referred to as KM). And while KM's principles include some, such as "fairness and honesty," that translate universally, there are others like "courtesy and humility" with components that feel out of place in US culture. How do you practice humility in a culture that values assertiveness? What is an American to make of "accord with natural laws" and "gratitude for blessings" as business principles?

At Matsushita in the US, people don't just brush off those values as irrelevant to American operations, but they aren't saddled with a set of unfamiliar do's and don'ts to fulfill them. The training department provides a half-day course based on the principles, in which – in typical American fashion – the participants are guided in interpreting for themselves what the principles mean to them.

So, to get back to humility, what do Americans do about that? Schupp says it does show up in the company culture. "You don't see people taking a lot of individual credit here," he maintains. "You hear a lot of 'we did it' instead of 'I did it.' When we put in a new HR information system, for example, it came in on time and within budget. The project team got the credit, not just the leader."

Probably the most obvious difference between Matsushita in the US and an indigenous American company is that there are a number of Japanese expatriates working there. At the top, the chairman is Japanese. Until recently there was an American president, but now instead of a president there is a strategic management council, made up of top officers who are split between Japanese and Americans. Of the company's three divisions, two are headed by Americans, and one by a Japanese. There are Japanese expatriates spread throughout the ranks too, often brought in to provide particular skills or expertise. All the expatriates aren't Japanese however. There are also some Europeans, on assignment from the company's European affiliates, again to provide missing expertise. Most expatriates are on three-to-five-year assignments.

The movement of employees goes both ways to a degree. The US company sends some employees to Japan for training, largely technical or production-related. There is also a new executive development program for top-level managers from around the world. Initiated and based in Japan, this program focuses on general management development through case studies, executive discussions, and visits to other companies to benchmark and compare. Participants have to be nominated to go, and the American subsidiary sends one or two a year.

Some Americans also travel to Japan to work, on assignment either to learn a particular skill on the job or to share one. A member of Schupp's staff was assigned to the Japanese training center in 2001 to share American training methods, "how we establish courses, our course content, what Americans expect from training." Schupp explains, "We use a lot of case studies and discussion. The traditional Japanese method is primarily lecture. So they know if they want to train foreign people in Japan, they need to adapt." The American isn't there just to instruct however. "She's also learning what courses they have that we could adopt here."

Japanese expatriates get training on American culture and customs both before they leave Japan and after they arrive in the US. "We teach them practices and customs in the US – different expectations for women, for example. We have women general managers here but in Japan you don't meet many women above lower levels." There's comparable training for Americans going to Japan, some of it focusing on the formality of Japanese etiquette – "where to stand in an elevator, where to sit in a car, how to eat." And there's also some training on Japanese customs and etiquette for American employees staying at home. Working for Matsushita, they do need to know things like where to seat people in meetings.

Going in either direction, or to/from Europe, expatriates' compensation is based upon their home country salaries, with offsets and allowances to take care of additional expenses and different tax and social security laws, as well as to maintain their home country retirement benefits.

What happens to an expatriate when an assignment is over varies somewhat between countries too. A Japanese returning home is guaranteed a job. In the US, Schupp says, returning expatriates can assume they'll get their old jobs or similar ones – if such a job is available. "That's all you can promise in America," he admits, "but we don't want to lose them when they come back. We're hoping to get something out of their experience, too."

INSIGHTS FROM MATSUSHITA

» Globalization doesn't have to mean homogenization.
» You can't impose a culture or a set of policies *created within one*.
» You can expect people to work by a set of values – if you allow them to define those values in their own cultural terms.
» Parent and subsidiary operations can learn from each other. Training programs can be an effective vehicle for this, as can work assignments.
» Expatriates need help adapting to strange new customs and practices. It helps to start the training before they move and to continue it in the new location.

ROYAL DUTCH/SHELL'S GLOBAL HR STRATEGY

For decades, Royal Dutch/Shell Group of Companies has been a model for other enterprises with global aspirations. Here, John Hofmeister, group HR director, outlines Shell's human resources strategic plan, designed to support the high growth expectations of Shell's businesses.

"We currently have identified seven key themes that drive Shell's people strategy.

"The first is attraction. How do we attract people from all the markets in the world? What's our way of branding ourselves to graduate hires or mature hires (people with five or more years of service). We have clear actions that we've decided to take: for example, we rarely sell ourselves as an oil and gas company. We sell ourselves as a consumer products company, as a technology company, as an energy company. Another part of our brand is that we are a renewable energy company: solar, hydrogen, and wind are part of our portfolio. So our attraction is to get people to think about Shell in very different ways instead of just thinking about drilling holes.

"Our second strategic theme is on-boarding – the process by which people join Shell or take a new job within Shell. On-boarding is critical because the most insecure moment a person has is when that person comes to a company or takes a new job within the company. We want people who are vulnerable to have a support system. So focusing on on-boarding addresses that period of vulnerability and lets vulnerable people know they are respected and cared about.

"That can mean, for example, training a manager in Nigeria how to be sensitive to the needs of a new employee, creating the employment contract early on so someone has a sense of purpose as early as possible. For a new hire, it also means building networks among other new people. We have a program called Shell Life – five days for newcomers to spend with other newcomers to learn about Shell, learn about themselves, learn about each other. On-boarding is also about something as basic as making sure the workplace is ready for a person the day that person arrives. We just brought somebody new into my office. A week before he arrived, his workstation was ready to go. On his first day, we had a little sign on his desk welcoming him, with flowers. That may sound simple, but I believe if you're going to be a successful global firm you'd better do the fundamentals well.

"The third area of strategy is our talent process. This is the whole chain of events from people planning (determining how many people and what kinds of backgrounds), to our recruiting process, movement of people through jobs, assessment and development of people, coaching and mentoring them, and ultimately up to and including succession planning. At Shell we've made assessment and development one word. We don't talk about assessment separate from development. We don't think of them as two different processes. You can't develop somebody who hasn't been assessed. Why would you assess people if you are not going to develop them? We don't assess people for the purpose of weeding them out.

"Nobody joins Shell without going through our assessment center process. Virtually all the people who are chosen through that process come out of the experience with a positive feeling. We build off that experience at four other career transition points in their careers: when they become first-time managers, lower middle managers, upper middle managers, and senior executives.

"Our fourth strategic area is diversity. We have a very clear action plan to ensure diversity as part and parcel of our entire HR value proposition, so that people from every culture feel included. We have only two targets. One is that 20% of our top executives will be women by 2008. We are currently at about 7% so we have a ways to go. Second: we will have 100% national cover of our top positions in each country in the world by 2004. What that means is that the top person in each country will be a local national – or could be a local national. It may turn out that we want to use those positions to develop other people, but our goal is to have a sufficiently robust talent base that we could have local nationals at the top in every country.

"Our target for developing women is quite rare among European companies. In fact many of our European company friends are not too happy we have it. One of the difficulties of promoting women is that the talent base is primarily British or American. Very few other countries have enabled the development of women to reach top levels, so it's really a dilemma because every time you end up promoting a senior woman, it tends to be American or British. But I think over 10 years this will change. So whether we make the 20% by 2008 is less important than if we have them in the pipeline.

If we never set a target we would never be better off than we are today. We've also been very clear to say we will continue to maintain the principles of meritocracy.

"We're creating a worldwide change agents' network to promote diversity. It includes 100 people around the world. Along with their regular jobs, they will also focus on making diversity real in their workplaces.

"The implementation of a diversity policy is a very big deal at Shell. At the end of each year, all 155 country managers will have to write letters confirming that the diversity policy is being practiced in their countries or report on areas where it is deficient. I don't think there is any other company in the world that does that.

"The fifth area of strategy is leadership education. We are committed to a leadership education program at each of the career transition points for managers: first time managers, lower middle, upper middle, and senior executive. There is other leadership education that occurs as well. We've hired the dean of a business school to head it up.

"The sixth area is communications. Our commitment is to have two-way communication with all staff on a monthly basis. We're just getting started with this and still defining the process. The goal is to engage all staff members every month in face-to-face communication with their manager, in a group setting, to exchange information. The process is a cascade from the group's center through the businesses. Businesses will add or shape messages for their operating units all around the world, so all staff will be informed of all issues that affect them and management will be informed of the views of staff. The reason we went this way is that our worldwide staff survey tells us statistically that the staff are not sufficiently well informed. They don't adequately understand all of the business parameters that affect them.

"Our last item of strategy is the creation of a Web-enabled worldwide human resource information system. We have agreed to spend a quarter of a billion dollars to do this over four years. It's a huge commitment. Each file will include all of an employee's evaluations over the years, the person's benefits choices, pay history, job history, and education history in the company. For an employee, accessing that information will be like using Web-enabled banking. The system will also help the company do organizational planning. How many geological engineers do we have all over the world? Today we don't have any quick way to assemble that information. We're going into the Sakhalin Island at the eastern-most end of Russia in a very big way. We need hundreds of people to go there. How do we assemble those people? Where do we get them from? How do we get them there? All that would be greatly facilitated with a worldwide HRIS. Or if we wanted to reorganize our commercial business in Europe, it would be much easier to look at organization scenarios with a system that showed all staff. Just as banks and financial institutions do all kinds of modeling with financial numbers, we'd like to do the same modeling with people instead of numbers.

"So all these seven elements work together to create a holistic people strategy that informs our business and group strategies. Our businesses have huge growth ambitions, and in our high-priced oil world we face endless growth prospects. We need people to make the growth happen. All of these strategies are designed to support the growth as well as the execution of Shell's businesses."

Author interview with John Hofmeister

QUESTIONS PROMPTED BY SHELL'S HR STRATEGY

The last thing you'd want to do is copy another company's HR strategy – not even Shell's. But the people strategy outlined by John Hofmeister does suggest some questions you should be asking yourself. Should some of these be high priority for your organization now?

» What are you doing to attract top talent and differentiate yourself from other companies recruiting from the same talent pool?
» Do you go out of your way to ensure that each new hire's first impression of your company is a good one, setting the stage for a positive long-term relationship?

» Do you firm up your talent base by regularly assessing people's skills and knowledge and providing appropriate developmental experiences?
» What are you doing to ensure that your company's top management group will reflect all the cultures in which you operate and include women as well as men?
» Do you provide leadership education at each transition point in your managers' careers?
» Are you ensuring that all staff throughout the world are well informed about the business and how goals and strategies affect them?
» Do you have an HRIS that provides HR professionals around the world with information on all employees worldwide?

Key Concepts and Thinkers

- » Words and phrases you should know
- » A framework for understanding cultures
- » People shaping the field of global HR.

This chapter is the quick guide to global human resources. It defines the key terms, encapsulates related concepts, and introduces some of the subject's pre-eminent thinkers.

GLOSSARY OF TERMS

Acquisition – One way for an enterprise to expand internationally, by purchasing an existing company in another country. For HR professionals this requires blending two social and corporate cultures, and often, figuring out how to replace a set of policies and practices geared to local laws and customs with another set whose origins were far away.

Balance sheet approach – An approach to compensating expatriates that links their base pay to their home country salary level, usually sweetened by an incentive to make the move and allowances for additional expenses and taxation.

Best practices – Those policies, processes, and behaviors that have been determined by benchmarking and surveys to be most effective at achieving the goals of a business function.

Bonus – Money paid by an employer to an employee, in addition to salary, when the organization or the individual meets or exceeds goals. Bonuses are often determined by percent of salary. Global companies may have consistent policies on bonuses across all their operations.

Capabilities – The key attributes, skills, fields of knowledge, and talents possessed by an organization or needed by it to fulfill its strategy.

Cultural sensitivity – An understanding of the differences in behaviors, attitudes, beliefs, and expectations that exist among different national, regional, and ethnic groups and a willingness to accommodate such differences. It's a crucial characteristic for living and working successfully in a country different from one's own. For more information, see "Understanding Cultural Differences" under "Related Concepts" later in this chapter.

Dual career couples – Married couples (or, interpreted more broadly, life partners) who are both employed. Dual career couples create a challenge for human resource professionals in international companies, since relocating an employee to another country usually means the non-assigned spouse has to quit work, losing income and disrupting that person's career.

E-learning – Defined broadly as education and training opportunities distributed via the Internet or through other computer or telecommunications technologies. Often more narrowly defined as Web-based training. Since these programs can be accessed by computer from anywhere in the world, providing a common experience for all participants, they are becoming an important part of the training and development offered by international companies.

Ethnocentric – One of three management orientations classified by Howard Perlmutter, it is characterized by strong parent country orientation and control. In ethnocentric companies, key positions throughout the world are filled by people recruited and developed in the home country.

Expatriate – A person living outside his or her native country (slang "expat").

Face – A state of dignity, usually referring to the avoidance of appearing to be wrong or to have made a mistake. In some cultures, saving face is a critical component of business and social relationships.

Geocentric – Third of Howard Perlmutter's management orientations, the geocentric mindset is the most truly global. Geocentric companies hire and develop the best people anywhere in the world and place them in key positions anywhere in the world, including membership in the worldwide management team. They also adopt best practices from wherever they find them, and balance global strategies with local practices.

Glass ceiling – A phrase used to describe a barrier, usually undocumented, that prevents certain people from rising to positions above a particular level in the organization. In US corporations, it usually refers to obstacles to advancement for minorities and women. In international enterprises it often refers to a barrier that keeps people from outside the parent country from the highest managerial ranks.

Global – Most precisely this refers to an attitude that transcends allegiances to national units. Used interchangeably with transnational, it is the final stage in a model known as the Stages of Internationalism. Truly global enterprises view the world not as a collection of national or regional markets but as one market. They produce wherever costs are lowest and quality highest, and deliver their goods and services wherever demand is highest. They seek resources – money, technology, people – wherever the best can be found. Their "headquarters" may be in their country of origin, may have relocated elsewhere, or may be split up into autonomous units. Global is also used, more liberally, to describe any company that has worldwide operations.

Going rate approach – An approach to compensating expatriates that links base salary to the going rate in the host country, not the home country.

HCN – Acronym for host country national. See below.

Host country national – A citizen of the country where a subsidiary is located, usually referring to a local employee of a company whose headquarters is in another country.

HRIS – Human resources information system; an integrated system to collect, store, and retrieve employee data used for making decisions about human resources. In some global companies the system can be accessed from around the world.

HR strategy – Plan for optimizing the use of people as a resource to support business strategy.

Inpatriate – Word used in some organizations for people from other countries working in the parent country.

LCN – Acronym for local country national. See "host country national."

Leadership brand – Attitudes and behaviors by leaders that support the company's core values, are modeled by top management, and are encouraged among leaders and potential leaders at all levels and in all locations. In international companies, the global leadership brand may be more of a philosophy, which is translated by people into locally appropriate behaviors.

Local country national – See "host country national."

Lump sum approach – An approach to expatriate compensation that includes a base salary and a lump sum to cover variables in housing, schools, etc. The employee determines how to allocate the money.

Mentor – In international companies, often a person who can not only provide guidance to an expatriate on handling the job abroad, but also helps the expatriate stay current and visible back home to avoid falling into the "out of sight, out of mind" syndrome.

MNE – Acronym for multinational enterprise. See below.

Multinational enterprise – Term generally used broadly to cover any organization with significant operations in locations other than the home country. It has largely replaced the term multinational corporation (MNC) in the literature.

Overseas subsidiary – A company that is majority or fully owned by an enterprise based in another country.

Parent country national – A citizen of the MNE's home country.

PCN – Acronym for parent country national. See above.

Performance management – A cycle of objective-setting, performance monitoring, and performance appraisal done on an annual or biannual basis. Widely accepted as advantageous for both management and employees in western countries, it does not always translate well in some countries where any form of feedback, positive or negative, is interpreted as insulting.

Personnel administration – Once commonly used name for what has evolved into the human resources department in most organizations. Theoretically at least, the name change is more than semantic. Personnel administration departments focused on administering programs for the care and feeding of employees. Human resource departments focus on people as an organizational resource and are concerned with maximizing the contribution they make to business strategy.

Polycentric – The second of three managerial orientations classified by Howard Perlmutter. It is characterized by strong host country control of subsidiary operations, which are staffed almost entirely by host country nationals.

Pre-departure training – Programs designed to help pending expatriates prepare for life and work in another country. Such training may include site visits by the candidate for relocation and spouse (or partner), orientation to the country and the culture for both employee and partner, job orientation, language training, and counseling on compensation, benefits, taxes, housing and other location-specific issues.

Repatriate – A returning expatriate. An issue for HR is that repatriates may find they have no job to come home to that either compares to their foreign assignment in terms of responsibility or matches the career progress their former colleagues have made while they were away or even that the company has reorganized and there is no job for them at all.

Stages of internationalization – The traditional steps on the way to becoming truly global:

1 pre-international or purely domestic;
2 exporting;
3 overseas production begins;
4 multinational operations, when foreign operations probably account for half or more of the company's sales and employment; and
5 transnational or global (see global above).

Strategic business partner – A unit within the organization that has a meaningful voice in establishing and implementing organizational strategy. Within the last decade, human resources has acquired this status in an increasing number of organizations.

Trailing spouse – The traditional term for a spouse who accompanies an employee on an assignment abroad.

TCN – Third country national. See below.

Third country national – An employee in an overseas subsidiary who is a citizen of a country other than the host country or the parent country. Some international companies transfer managers and technical experts from one subsidiary to another, creating a cadre of third country nationals who move around the world. A shortage of labor in a host country can also lead to importing labor from other countries, giving rise to another group of TCNs.

Transnational – See global above.

"Think globally, act locally" – A maxim for doing business abroad. It calls for pursuing a global strategy while following the customs and laws of each location where the company operates. It's a balancing act all companies struggle with.

Variable pay – A compensation system in which at least part of the employee's pay varies depending upon the performance of the individual and/or the organization in achieving goals. While it is customary in some countries, it is strongly resisted in others.

Works councils – Chiefly in Europe, employee groups elected within a company, empowered to consult with management, negotiate grievances, and participate in decision making.

Work permit – Documentation required to work in a foreign country.

RELATED CONCEPTS

Operating successfully through people in other countries always comes down to one thing: the ability to understand and work within a different culture. It's hard when people behave in ways you were taught were wrong, and when they fault you for doing things you've always been encouraged to do. It's easier if you understand the mindset from which they operate and recognize that it's valid, just different. The cultural concepts described below help put those mindsets into perspective.

Unlocking cultural differences

One of the best ways to unlock the mysteries of cultural variations is through the framework developed by Geert Hofstede of the Netherlands. Here are Hofstede's five "Cultural Value Dimensions."[1]

1 *Power Distance*, defining employees' response to and expectations of those in authority.

   In high power distance cultures, bosses tend to be more autocratic and employees expect to be told what to do. In low power distance cultures, employees expect their bosses to consult with them before making decisions. (Based on research he did in the 1960s and 70s, Hofstede identified Latin America, France, Spain, and most Asian and African countries as regions with high power distance cultures, and the US, Britain, and most northern European countries as low power distance.)

   Imagine how that difference in perspective changes the response to the American management dictum: don't bring me problems, bring me solutions. In the US, it's meant to be empowering, assuring employees that their managers respect their problem-solving ability, and give them the authority to take corrective actions. But in a high-power distance culture, employees interpret such a management attitude as abandonment, or worse, an invitation to hide, rather than report, problems.

2 *Individualism/Collectivism*, or "Which comes first, me or the team?"

   People in individualistic cultures expect to take care of themselves and make decisions based on their own needs. In collectivist cultures, people value loyalty to the group, base decisions on the group's needs, and expect the group to take care of them. (Among countries with individualistic cultures, Hofstede placed the US, Canada, France, and South Africa. He identified Japan, Mexico, and Greece, for example, as countries with collectivist cultures.)

Although they are competitive, individualists do work well together on a team when they perceive the team's goals to be complementary to their own and anticipate that the team's success will contribute to their own advancement. Collectivists identify with the team's goals and co-operate to achieve them.

3 *Masculinity/Femininity*, a measurement of whether people in a culture are motivated more strongly by the more "masculine" goals of achievement, advancement, and recognition, or by the more "feminine" pursuits of co-operation, security, and good relationships. (Hofstede rated Great Britain, the US, and Japan among the highest on masculinity. Sweden, France, and Indonesia were among the top-ranked countries on the femininity scale.)

The masculine and feminine labels may be less politically correct now than they were when Hofstede did his original research back in the 1960s and 70s, but cultures still exhibit the characteristics the words were used to define.

4 *Uncertainty Avoidance*, an expression of people's comfort in situations where the outcome is unknown.

In cultures that rank high on uncertainty avoidance, people prefer to live by rules and structures that minimize the occurrence of unexpected results. People with low uncertainty avoidance place more value on the opportunity for innovation and creativity than on the assurance of guaranteed results, and may even be energized by the risks inherent in a project with an uncertain outcome. (Hofstede's research placed Korea, Japan, and Latin America high on the uncertainty avoidance scale and the US, The Netherlands, and Great Britain among those countries on the low end.)

5 *Long-term/Short-term Orientation*, which is about the willingness to make trade-offs between short and long-term gratification. (China, Japan, and India rated high among countries having cultures with long-term orientation and Great Britain, Canada, and Germany were among countries with short-term orientation.)

KEY THINKERS

Steve Kerr

Say the words "leadership development" and the first name that comes to lips of everyone in the HR field is Steve Kerr. The prime architect of the modern curriculum at GE's famous Crotonville education center and the force behind GE's much-copied work-outs, Dr. Kerr was chief learning officer and vice president of leadership development at GE from 1989 until 2001. He is now chief learning officer and a managing director at the Goldman Sachs Group, headquartered in New York.

Previously, Dr. Kerr was dean of the University of Southern California business school and had been on the faculties of Ohio State University and the University of Michigan. He is co-author (with Ron Ashkenas, Todd Jick, Dave Ulrich) of the book *The Boundaryless Organization* (Jossey-Bass, 1995) and editor of *Ultimate Rewards* (Harvard Business School Press, 1997).

To be a global leader, says Dr. Kerr, requires one characteristic that leaders in domestic companies may never have to think about. That is cultural awareness and sensitivity.

"You become a successful organization by having a set of beliefs," Dr. Kerr explains. "That's fairly easy within one culture. But when you go outside to other cultures, they will challenge everything you believe to be true. On the one hand, you don't want to be an ugly American. On the other hand, you can't be a chameleon and make your own culture disappear every time you go out of town."

Dr. Kerr elaborates with an example. "In America, we think hiring based on merit is good; nepotism and cronyism are bad. But in Thailand, they do nepotism and cronyism. So a Thai guy says to me, 'Look at this through my eyes. You have an important job to fill, you post it, and you hire a stranger to do it. I'd hire my cousin. I've known him for 30 years. I know he won't let me down. He won't cheat me.' You leave the room thinking, 'Why don't I hire my cousin?' It gets bewildering," he adds. "It's really subtle and it's no small part of leadership."

Some issues cut even deeper into the heart of leadership principles. "What do you do if you go into a country and are told it will take seven years to get a telephone?" he asks, and adds, "Then they tell you they

have a system called 'expedited payments.' What do you do then about
your policy of no bribes?''

''All you can do,'' Dr. Kerr concludes, ''is help people understand
the tension. Sometimes you walk away from business. Sometimes you
do it the Rome way. You have to trust bright people to make these
decisions.''

Mike Losey

Before his recent retirement as president and CEO of the Society
for Human Resource Management (SHRM), Mike Losey spearheaded
a drive to expand the size and influence of the group worldwide,
resulting in a three-fold increase in membership to more than 150,000
over 10 years. He's also served as president of the World Federation
of Personnel Management Associations and as president of the North
American Human Resource Management Association. So he is one of
the best-known figures among human resource professionals.

Losey also spent many years in corporate HR, including a lengthy
stint at Sperry Corporation. He is co-editor (with Dave Ulrich) of
Tomorrow's HR Management: 48 Thought Leaders Call for Change
(Wiley, 1997).

If you ask Mike Losey (as the author did) what differentiates global
HR from domestic HR, he'll turn the question around to remind you of
all the things that are pretty much the same. ''I like to identify what's
similar, to build confidence,'' he says. ''Then we need to explain what's
different.''

Losey maintains that business around the world increasingly mirrors
what is done in HR in the United States – such as increasing communication with employees and diversity in the workplace. He also points
out that the processes of recruiting, selection, job interviewing, and
training are much the same everywhere. Health, safety and security are
also very similar.

Then he goes into the differences. ''When you get to compensation,
there are major differences,'' Losey notes, and gives an example, ''You
can't just give a Japanese salesperson an incentive plan and have it
work.'' And there is more to it than just determining salaries. ''You
have to understand inflation and indexing.'' Benefits are different, too.
In Germany, for example, it would be against the law to link vacation
to years of service.

He also describes differences among unions in various parts of the world. In Europe, unions are affiliated with political parties; in the US they are defined by industry, and in Japan by company. "In Germany there are two unions, in the US about 250, and in Japan 20,000." But in Germany both unions will be represented in one company. "So you have two unions with very different mentalities. Can you imagine trying to get them to agree for collective bargaining?" he asks. "That would be like trying to negotiate with the Republican and the Democrats at the same time."

Despite the differences, Losey says if you are a good HR person in your home country and can adapt reasonably well, you have the capacity to be outstanding globally. Hopefully he's right, because global is in most HR professionals' futures.

"I had one person call me from Kennedy airport on the way to Hong Kong saying, 'Can you tell me all I need to know about Hong Kong?'" Losey recalls. "That's how most people get into global. They don't think about it. All of a sudden they are in it. There are very few companies today that don't deal globally."

Vladimir Pucik

Vladimir Pucik, professor of international human resources at the International Institute for Management Development (IMD) at Lausanne, Switzerland, doesn't buy into global HR's favorite slogan: think globally; act locally. He says it should be the other way around.

"Customers are very local. They don't want to be homogenized; they want to be treated as individuals. So companies need to be asking: "How do I understand local customer needs?" In order to do that, they need to think locally. But in order to compete they need to act globally, utilizing resources and capabilities worldwide."

To illustrate he tells a story about the Finnish mobile communications firm Nokia (which he admits may be more legend than exact truth). It seems some Nokia people were traveling in Asia when they noticed fishermen using mobile phones to check on the price of fish that day. Subsistence level fishermen did not in any way match the market Nokia had targeted for its phones, leading the Nokia people to realize there were a lot of market opportunities open to them if they started thinking from a local perspective. "You could never figure this out in Helsinki," Dr. Pucik points out.

In this kind of local/global environment, he says, HR needs to deal with three key issues.

First, how do we build a mindset that can deal with the contradictions of the global business? The global-local bifurcation is only one of the dilemmas Dr. Pucik raises. He lists other seemingly contradictory needs: exploiting existing resources vs. building future capabilities; creating learning alliances with competitors; lowering costs vs. meeting customer expectations; change management vs. stability and continuity; encouraging innovation and risk-taking vs. minimizing failures.

Second, how can HR specifically contribute to the competitive ability of the firm? Historically, Dr. Pucik reminds us, companies could delegate decision making to top management. With only a few products, a few markets, and a stable environment, that worked. But with multiple products, global markets, and changing conditions, you can't delegate upward or you'll be too late to be competitive. So you have to create an environment where people can communicate with each other and make decisions. The purpose of empowerment, he asserts, isn't to do something nice for employees, it's to strengthen the firm. HR has a unique responsibility to be the architect of such organizations.

Third, how do you manage performance and develop talent in a global setting? Dr. Pucik stresses the importance of a performance management process that measures both using resources effectively now and building future capabilities. The challenge is in applying it in a consistent way around the world. "If you have a Chinese subsidiary, an Italian affiliate, and an American one, you have to make sure they are all looking at performance in the same way."

He says it's possible to achieve this without stomping on cultural differences. "People say you have to be careful about different subordinate/superior relationships in different cultures. But you can do 360 degree feedback in China, too. Chinese employees have opinions of their bosses. The question is how to collect the information. The process might not be one hundred percent the same, but what counts is the outcome."

Vladimir Pucik is co-author (with Paul Evans) of *The Global Challenge: Frameworks for International Human Resource Management* (McGraw Hill/Irwin, Jan. 2002); *Accelerating International Growth*

(Wiley, 2001); and editor of *Globalizing Management: Creating and Leading the Competitive Organization* (Wiley, 1993). He has been on the faculties of Cornell University and the University of Michigan, and was a visiting scholar at Keio and Hitotsubashi University in Tokyo.

Dave Ulrich

Author, consultant, and professor of business administration at the University of Michigan, Dave Ulrich has been described by *Business Week* as one of the world's top ten management educators and the top educator in HR. His books include *Results-Based Leadership* (co-author) (Harvard Business School Press, 1999); *Human Resource Champions: The Next Agenda for Adding Value and Delivering Results* (Harvard Business School Press, 1997); *Tomorrow's HR Management: 48 Thought Leaders Call for Change* co-editor (with Mike Losey) (Wiley, 1997); and *The Boundaryless Organization* (co-author – see Kerr above) (Jossey-Bass, 1995).

In an interview with HBS Press, Dr. Ulrich described the role of human resources as four-fold: "strategic partner + administrative expert + employee champion + change agent ... strategic partners align HR systems with business strategy and set HR priorities for a business entity; administrative experts save their businesses money through more efficient design and delivery of HR systems; employee champions ensure that employee contributions to the business remain high in terms of both employee commitment and competence; change agents help businesses through transformations and to adapt to changing business conditions. The true HR business partner must manage the paradox of business results *and* employee commitment; change *and* stability. Learning to master these paradoxes will be the essence of the HR of the future."[2]

When he talks about global enterprises, it is also in terms of another paradox. "You have to allow local autonomy and adapt to local conditions, and at the same time get global leverage for economy of scale and efficiency." Companies are constantly under dual pressures for global integration and local responsiveness.

Responding to both pressures requires companies to "figure out what they can leverage globally – things like brand and technology, what John Kenneth Galbraith called back room. Then they can adapt the front room things, such as things that touch the consumer."

Another way Dr. Ulrich suggests for beginning to resolve the question of what should be consistent globally and what can be adapted locally is to determine what is core and what is not core to the organization.[3] So, for example, acting decisively and quickly might be core to the organization. But as long as the result is quick and effective action, the style used to get there may not be core. In fact it could take a different form in Japan, where it might mean getting a team together quickly, and in the US, where it could mean taking quick action on one's own decision.

Dr. Ulrich likes to look at organizations as bundles of capabilities. Once a company has determined its global strategy, its next task is not to organize to implement that strategy but to identify the capabilities it will need to put its strategy into practice. With the capabilities identified, it is HR's job to make the appropriate investments to ensure those capabilities exist. So, when Intel decided to make a strategic shift to focus on customers rather than product development, HR recruited people with that mindset, developed training that focused on customers, and created incentive programs to reward customer-oriented behavior.[4]

But recognizing what customers want and choosing the right rewards to provide incentives for employees probably has to be adapted locally. "Often, a global HR strategy is a principle," Dr. Ulrich says. "The practice and application of that principle have to be adapted at a local level."

NOTES

1 Hofstede, G. (1996) *Culture and Organizations: Software of the Mind*. McGraw-Hill, New York.
2 Quoted from www.hbsp.harvard.edu/products/press/trans/qa_ulrich.html.
3 Ulrich elaborates on this and other global capabilities in "The New Frontier of Global HR," co-authored with J. Stewart Black as a chapter for an upcoming book, tentatively called *Practicing International HR*, edited by Richard Goff.
4 "The New Frontier of Global HR." (See [3] above.)

Resources

- » Comprehensive books, gurus' books, and books with a narrow focus
- » Magazines, both paper and online
- » Classic and current articles
- » Information services
- » Best sites for Web surfers.

Global human resources covers a lot of territory – and not just geographically. Do you want to know about HR planning and strategy development in multinational enterprises? Do you need information on compensation and benefits practices around the world? Perhaps you need fast information on labor laws in countries you've barely heard of. Or maybe you want help easing the expatriation/repatriation of your globe-trotting employees. The sweep of global HR goes from law to psychology – and covers myriad business practices in between.

The goal of this chapter is to point you toward useful resources whether you need a broad overview or you want to zero in on details relating to a specific HR function. It covers books, periodicals, specific articles, information services, and pertinent Websites.

BOOKS

To help you find what you need, this section is divided into three categories: comprehensive overviews, what the gurus are saying, and narrower focus (books that deal with only one topic within the HR family).

Comprehensive overviews

» Briscoe, D.R. (1995) *International Human Resource Management*. Prentice Hall, Upper Saddle River, NJ.

If you need an introduction to the broad scope of global HR, this book provides it. Used as a textbook in university courses, it covers the field from staffing to labor relations. While its examples look a bit dated when you check the reference notes, the issues are still current. You may have to look for a used copy or check with your library, because, according to Amazon.com, it has just gone out of print.

» Dowling, P.J., Welch, D.E., & Schuler, R.S. (1999) *International Human Resource Management: Managing People in a Multinational Context*, 3rd edn. South-Western, Cincinnati, OH.

This is another textbook that covers the full range of global HR functions. In addition, it focuses in on human resource practices in China and India. The fundamentals are all there, and the examples are newer than in the Briscoe book, but the writing style is more academic.

What the gurus are saying

The books in this section may not have the words global or international in their titles, but their authors or editors are among the most respected thinkers in the field of global HR. So what they are saying about HR in general will have broad applicability wherever you practice.

» Gratton, L. (2000) *Living Strategy: Putting People at the Heart of Corporate Purpose*. Financial Times Prentice Hall, Upper Saddle River, NJ.

   Lynda Gratton is dean of the full-time MBA program at the London Business School, one of the leading international business schools. This book investigates both the line manager's role and the human resource role in creating a living strategy, which incorporates the human perspective on time, the search for meaning in organizations, and engaging the soul of the organization.

» Ulrich, D. (1997) *Human Resource Strategy: The Next Agenda for Adding Value and Delivering Results*. Harvard Business School Press, Boston.

   In this book, Ulrich identifies four separate roles that human resource professionals must play to meet current and future challenges – including globalization. These roles are strategic partner, administrative expert, employee champion, and change agent. For more works by Dave Ulrich, see "Key Thinkers" in Chapter 8: "Key Concepts and Thinkers."

» Ulrich, D., Losey, M., & Lake, G., eds. (1997) *Tomorrow's HR Management: 48 Thought Leaders Call for Change*. Wiley, New York.

   This book is a compendium of insights from 48 respected HR executives, consultants, and scholars from around the world, who offer their views on the future of the field and recommend courses of action to increase HR's productivity, efficiency, and adaptability – the latter a particularly critical characteristic for operating in a global context.

Books for and about expatriates

» Black, J.S., ed. (1999) *Globalizing People Through International Assignments*. Addison-Wesley, Boston MA.

This book is a guide to selecting and training people to go abroad, supporting and assessing them while they are there, and repatriating them successfully.

» Black, J.S. & Gregersen, H.B. (1998) *So You're Going Overseas*. Global Business Publisher, San Diego CA.

A step-by-step handbook for preparing to take an international assignment. It's for people going abroad and for trainers whose job it is to get them ready to go. There are two companion workbooks , *So You're Going Overseas: Employee Workbook* (1998) and *So You're Going Overseas: Spouse Workbook* (1998) with tips, checklists and exercises.

» Black, J.S. & Gregersen, H.B. (1999) *So You're Coming Home*. Global Business Publisher, San Diego CA.

A natural follow-up to *So You're Going Overseas*, this handbook focuses on the repatriation process, which many people find a surprisingly difficult readjustment.

Compensation and benefits

» Reynolds, C. (1999) *2000 Guide to Global Compensation and Benefits*. Harcourt, New York.

Five sections include an overview, a guide to designing global compensation to meet your company's needs, a discussion of government social security programs and corporate benefits programs worldwide, summaries of compensation and benefits practices in different regions of the world, and challenges ahead. The book also points the reader to additional sources of information.

Culture

» Hofstede, G. (1996) *Culture and Organizations: Software of the Mind*. McGraw-Hill, New York.

Based on decades of research, Hofstede offers five cultural value dimensions to explain the different perceptions, expectations, and behaviors of people in different societies.

» Trompenaars, F. & Hampden-Turner, C. (1997) *Riding The Waves of Culture: Understanding Diversity in Global Business*. McGraw-Hill, New York.

The authors describe four basic types of corporate culture: The Family (Japan, Belgium) The Eiffel Tower (France, Germany) The Guided Missile (US, UK) The Incubator (Silicon Valley). The book also recommends ways for managers to build the cross-cultural skills, sensitivity, and awareness needed to succeed in cultures other than their own.

Labor laws

» Keller, W.L. (2000) *International Labor and Employment Laws*. BNA Books, Washington, D.C.

Examines labor and employment laws of the European Union and in selected member countries, NAFTA and its member countries, and a selection of other countries. There's also a section on international organizations.

PERIODICALS

The following periodicals focus exclusively on global HR or cover human resources in general, and frequently carry articles devoted to global issues.

Global HR

Formerly *HR World*, this is a monthly publication for senior HR decision-makers in multinational enterprises, covering strategic and policy issues. Recent editions have included articles on work/life balances around the world and accommodating religious beliefs. It is published in the UK by Reed Business, and you can request a free copy or subscribe online at www.readbusiness.com. *Global HR* is also distributed to members of the SHRM Global Forum and you can read selected articles on that organization's Website, www.shrmglobal.org.

HR Magazine

The official publication of the Society for Human Resource Management (SHRM), this magazine is primarily for HR professionals in the United States, but it does periodically include good articles on global issues. Recent editions have looked at worldwide terrorism and cultural sensitivity. You don't have to be an SHRM member to subscribe, and you can read selected articles free online at www.shrm.com.

HRProfessional

The membership magazine for the Human Resources Professionals of Ontario (HRPAO), *HRProfessional*'s focus is primarily Canadian, but it carries articles on global issues too. Recent ones have included "Compensation Strategies for International Assignments" and "Winning Away From Home: The HR role in overseas work assignments." You don't have to be an HRPAO member to subscribe, and you can read selected articles free online at www.hrprofessional.org.

Human Resources Management International Digest

An Emerald journal, published in the UK by MCB University Press, this digest prints abridged versions of articles from HR publications in 120 countries around the world. It appears seven times a year. Find out about subscribing at www.emeraldinsight.com/journals/hrmid/sub info.htm.

International HR Journal

Published in the United States by the West Group, this quarterly journal analyzes issues facing companies operating in foreign markets. Its purpose is to keep subscribers up-to-date and competitive on all aspects of international HR management. You can read a sample chapter and get subscription information at www.hr-esource.com.

People Management

The membership magazine for the Chartered Institute of Personnel and Development (CIPD) in the UK, *People Management*'s focus is primarily on HR issues in the UK and Ireland, but it carries news on international issues too, particularly pan-European topics. You don't have to be a CIPD member to subscribe, and you can read articles free online at www.peoplemanagement.co.uk.

SHRM Global Perspective

You have to be a member of the Society for Human Resource Management (SHRM) and the SHRM Global Forum to get this bi-monthly newsletter that is devoted to global HR issues. Whether it's focused on Internet recruiting or dealing with bullies at work, the newsletter conscientiously avoids any US bias. You can order a free sample copy or find out about membership at www.shrmglobal.org.

T+D Magazine

The flagship publication of the American Society for Training and Development (ASTD), *T+D Magazine* sometimes carries articles that focus on global issues in training. Two recent ones were "Developing Globally Literate Learners" and "Global E-warming," which described the increasing popularity of e-learning in countries around the world. You can read selected articles online or find out about subscribing at www.astd.org.

Workforce

Published in the Unites States, this magazine about HR trends and tools sometimes includes articles on global HR issues. The April 1998 issue was devoted to global topics, and the articles in it are still worth checking out. You can do that in the archives at www.workforce.com, where you can read the entire publication free or subscribe to get it in your mailbox each month.

Worldlink

This is the official quarterly newsletter of the World Federation of Personnel Management Associations. It contains news and features on trends and developments in employment and HR-related practices around the world. You can read the latest issue online at www.wfpma.com/pubs.html or get paper copies through your national association.

ARTICLES WORTH TRACKING DOWN

Classics

These articles offer more than historical interest. If you change the dates and inflate the dollar numbers sprinkled throughout, you could be reading something written this year. That's the scary part. Reading them gives you a sense of how deeply entrenched the global issues really are.

» Clee, G.H. and di Scipio, A. "Creating a World Enterprise," *Harvard Business Review*. Nov-Dec, 1959.

International investments by corporations had just taken off in a big way when this article appeared. Its premise is "centralize responsibility for strategic planning and control; decentralize responsibility for 'local' planning and operations." There are plenty of examples of companies accomplishing that feat and of others struggling to achieve it.

» Perlmutter, H.V. "The Tortuous Evolution of the Multinational Corporation," *Columbia Journal of World Business*. Jan-Feb, 1969.

This article presents Permutter's 3-style model to describe the relationships between headquarters and subsidiaries in international organizations. Whole companies or specific functions within companies are defined as ethnocentric (home country orientation), polycentric (host country orientation), and geocentric (world orientation).

Recent and current

» Black, J.S. & Gregersen, H.B. "The right way to manage expats," *Harvard Business Review*, March-April, 1999.

The authors maintain that too many companies get anemic returns on their investment in sending employees on international assignments. They prescribe a three-phase approach to sending people for the right reasons, sending the right people, finishing the right way.

» "Global HR Leaders Agenda," *HR World* (now *GlobalHR*), March-April, 2000.

The results of a survey sponsored by Cendant International Assignment Services, in association with *HR World* and the International Institute of Human Resources (now SHRM Global Forum). Fifty HR executives in leading multinational enterprises participated in the survey, which focused on emerging trends in the profession and the skills these leaders consider essential for success. A number of prominent authors contributed to the analysis of the results in this article, which also includes brief interviews with some of the surveyed executives. Look for the article online at www.shrmglobal.org/publications/hrworld/leaders.htm.

» Quelch, J.A. and Bloom, H. "Ten Steps to a Global Human Resource Strategy," *Strategy & Business*, 1st quarter, 1999.

This is a how-to for hiring high-potential managerial talent in every part of the world where your company operates, developing and retaining them, and building an organization that takes advantage of their capabilities and provides them with opportunities to rise to the top.

» Roberts, B. "Going Global," *HR Magazine*, August, 2000.

Hot on every HR department's lists of must-do's is build a global human resource management system. This article is about the issues and pitfalls you need to prepare for as you undertake this enormous, costly project.

» Wellins, R. & Rioux, S. "The Growing Pains of Globalizing HR," *Career Journal* from the *Wall Street Journal* (www.careerjournal.com), reprinted from *T+D Magazine*.

Report on the results of a survey, "Globalization of HR Practices," conducted by Developmental Dimensions International. The survey involved 206 companies. The article reports on the companies' top priorities: leadership development, performance management, and recruitment of high-quality employees. It also describes the top global challenges: worldwide variations, varying perceptions of the value of HR, and resistance to change. Finally, it describes what some companies are doing to create a consistent culture worldwide. Look for this article online at the url above.

INFORMATION SERVICES

Worldwatch

You must be a member of SHRM Global Forum to access Worldwatch's online services, which include Country Guides: country-by-country packages of information culled from embassies and consulates, official government resources on labor and employment laws, academic institutions, HR organizations, newspapers, and job banks, as well as general country information from travel guides and tourism offices. Worldwatch also offers information on worldwide employment laws and Country Profiles from Watson Wyatt Worldwide. Get information at www.shrmglobal.org/worldwatch/index.htm.

WEBSITES WORTH VISITING

Remember, one good Website leads to another, so this selection of sites should point you to many more.

www.expatforum.com

Point your expatriate employees here to join online discussion groups with others like themselves. There are active strings of messages on a variety of topics dealing with a range of countries. The site is sponsored by the consulting firm, HR International.

www.learningcircuits.com

American Society for Training & Development's site for e-learning. It's loaded with articles and they are all free.

www.recruitsoft.com

If you are doing any Internet-based recruiting – and what company isn't? – this is a good source of information about how companies are recruiting from their own corporate Websites.

www.shrm.org

Yes, this is the Website of a US organization. But it has terrific links to sister organizations all over the world, to just about every publication that deals with HR subjects, and a variety of other related sites. It's a good place to start to do Web research.

www.shrmglobal.org

SHRM's Global Forum is all about global HR. You have to be a member to access a lot of what's offered on this Website, but not all. There are links to publications that cover global HR in general and others that focus on specific disciplines such as compensation and benefits. There are also links to a variety of other Websites that offer information you can use.

www.ssa.gov/international/inter_intro.html

Straightening out the social security situation of expatriates can be tricky. This US Government site explains the bilateral social security agreements between the United States and 18 other countries. If you are sending employees to or from the US, it's worth looking at.

www.wfpma.com

Website of the World Federation of Personnel Management Associations, this site provides information about the Federation and its country affiliates. Links to the newsletter *Worldlink* and an HR competencies report appear on the site. Hopefully these links will be working better by the time you try to access them.

www.windhamworld.com

This site provides annual global relocation trends surveys, covering the expatriate population, expatriate sources and destinations, global business strategy, and cross-cultural training. It's the Website of GMAC Global Relocation Services/Windham International. That organization sponsors the survey along with the National Foreign Trade Council and SHRM Global Forum.

Ten Steps to Making it Work

» Business
» Balance
» Strategy
» People
» Technology.

Global human resources isn't just one function; it's a related group of
functions, all of them focused on making the most of the most powerful
resource organizations have – people. Each of these functions has a
specialized body of knowledge and requires its own set of sophisticated
skills. Every day that knowledge is growing, as are the skills required to
apply it. So it would be frivolous to suggest that there are just 10 steps
that, followed faithfully and in sequence, promise world class results
in the application of all the functions. This is especially true since not
only is the definition of "world class" still evolving, but ironically, it
must be as credible on a local scale in China, for example, or Nigeria
or Australia, as on a global balance sheet.

Still, drawing from the company experiences described in previous
chapters of this book, it is possible and valuable to identify a set of
best practices that instruct all the functions. Some of these are things
the best companies have been doing differently from the also-rans for
a long time. Others are procedures or behaviors that are new even for
them – practices that they have identified as the right course to embark
on now.

1. BECOME AN EXPERT ON YOUR COMPANY'S BUSINESS AND ITS GLOBAL MARKET

It's not enough to know everything there is to know about compensation or labor relations or management development, or even to have
broad knowledge of all of these and other human resource functions.
That's the old personnel administration way – to focus exclusively
on the people-maintenance tasks, leaving the business side to operations and finance. Operating that way, it didn't matter a lot whether
the employer was in the business of producing widgets or curing
cancer.

But that attitude contributed to the perception in the operations
and financial sides of the business, and ironically even among many
individual employees, that personnel was essentially a pain in the neck,
more concerned about filling out forms than facilitating results. While
it was a pain in the neck, it was also perceived, with a sigh, to be
a necessary one. But thanks to the Internet and to external service
centers, many companies are discovering it is no longer necessary to
tolerate the eternal crick.

HR's new job is more challenging: not just to keep track of people, but to maximize their contribution to the business success of the organization. It's HR's responsibility to help the organization define the capabilities it needs to implement its business strategies in the global marketplace, and then to build a worldwide organization of people capable and motivated to support those competencies. Now, to fulfill HR's role, it does matter what the business is. The capabilities for making widgets and selling them around the world are far different from those for healthcare research.

In a nutshell, being a strategic business partner requires knowing the business.

2. MANAGE THE GLOBAL/LOCAL BALANCE

In theory it should be relatively easy to separate core values – those things that must be held constant around the globe – from behaviors – the way people in different cultures express those values. But in reality, it's not so easy. Is pay for performance a value? Or is it a western-culture manifestation of a broader value of fairness, which in Japan leads to differentiating salaries not by performance but by the needs of the employee and consideration of factors like the size of the family the employee must support?

Here's an easier one: no bribes. Lots of international countries put that explicitly in their statements of values or basic principles. That's pretty straightforward until you want to set up shop in a country where it's going to take seven years to get a telephone unless you abide by the local system of "expedited payments." Is it a bribe or simply a local business practice? Not so easy after all, is it?

Managing the global/local tension requires comparing local practices and traditions to each of the company's core values/principles and deciding which are valid cultural differences and which, if any, do violate the principles that make the company what it is. Some decisions accommodate a wide variety of local practices. Some may keep you from even setting up shop in a particular country. And in some cases, you may define your value narrowly and require adherence to it even in cultures where it is not the norm. That's a tough road to follow, but it can be done. Royal Dutch/Shell effectively uses a globally consistent assessment process even in countries where any performance feedback is viewed as criticism and saving face is a cultural must. Shell succeeds by preparing people for it from the start: recruits go through an assessment center before they are hired.

Don't expect to achieve a sharp line that forever differentiates between what's global and what's local. There will always be gray areas that will require review and negotiation. Continued informed dialogue will always be key.

3. DEVELOP A GLOBAL HR STRATEGY THAT SUPPORTS THE BUSINESS STRATEGY

When you know the organization's global business strategy, the capabilities required to fulfill it, and the values that will shape all decisions worldwide, you have the components for creating a global human resources strategy. This strategy focuses on principles and practices that will be consistent worldwide, and in that way informs and guides the translation of the strategy into local tactics. (For an account of Royal Dutch/Shell's global strategy, see Chapter 7: In Practice.)

4. PUT TRANSACTIONAL ACTIVITIES ONLINE

The technology exists to keep employee records on Web-accessible databases, let employees determine and change their benefits choices online, allow employees to sign up for training via the Internet/intranet, and keep training records the same way. So go ahead. Let technology relieve you of paper pushing. You've got better things to do.

5. PROMOTE MULTICULTURAL DIVERSITY

Any company that aspires to serve a world market gives itself a head start by building an organization, at all levels, that looks as international as its marketplace. The reason is simple: it is just good business. Consultant Warren Wilhelm describes working with a group in a large Swiss banking concern. "Seated around the table were ten people, eight of whom were from countries other than Switzerland. They didn't have an easy, congenial relationship because they all came at the problem from different perspectives. But by the time they thrashed it out they had a better answer."

For multiculturalism to work, people not only need the opportunity to work abroad, they also need these two supports.

» *Education about other cultures they will interact with and training in how to behave appropriately*. Matsushita of Japan and its US subsidiary have cultural sensitivity training on both sides of the Pacific. Before leaving Japan for a US assignment, Japanese expatriates receive training in how to work with Americans, covering American laws and regulations as well as practices and customs. In the US, Americans traveling to Japan get comparable training. And the US company builds awareness among all its employees of Japanese customs and etiquette. There is also an exchange program, whereby the two companies swap people for a limited period of time to give them a cultural immersion experience.

» *Role models who clearly and visibly respect and appreciate the difference among people*. At Shell, group HR director John Hofmeister says, "Some of our most senior executives are Asian. There is no impatience in dealing with their accents or the way they convey messages. It's just natural and the flow of the company that the way people talk and the way they behave is going to be according to a national origin that they reflect. We have some very senior Nigerians. Nigerians can act and talk differently from people in Europe or from the US. People just naturally wait for them to explain. You must have an appreciation for Nigerian culture to know where they are coming from."

6. MAKE IT WORTHWHILE TO TAKE INTERNATIONAL ASSIGNMENTS

Companies will tell you how important it is for their leaders to have international experience. Yet Americans in particular have a reputation for not wanting to pull up stakes and move to another country. One reason is that for them reality doesn't reflect the expressed value. In fact, in many companies, very few among the top management team have worked abroad. And managers or professionals who do take overseas assignments are often passed over for promotions at home, falling into an "out-of-sight, out-of-mind" vacuum.

One way to change the situation might be a sweeping policy change making international experience a requirement for top management positions. But that would probably be ineffective until the organization had developed a pool of qualified people to move into the upper ranks.

A good place to start is by preparing people for repatriation from the time they contemplate taking an overseas assignment. Having a mentor at home to keep the expatriate up to date on what's happening there, and to keep the expatriate's memory alive in the home office can help. Even better is a career development plan that plots out future options for high potential people two or three career moves in advance. After a decade or so of being told they are responsible for their own careers, most people aren't looking for an iron-clad promise. What they do expect is a commitment on the part of the organization to value their international experience and give them an opportunity to use the new knowledge and skills they've learned.

These days an overseas move often has to be worthwhile not just for employees, but for their spouses who have their own careers to worry about. How do you make it worthwhile for a spouse to quit a good job and put all career aspirations on the back burner to move to a country that may not even grant the person a work permit? So far, the best practices companies have discovered include job search support and funds for career development. No one's found the perfect solution yet, but the best companies are working hard at it.

7. OPEN TOP MANAGEMENT RANKS TO LOCAL NATIONALS

The ideal is an executive team that reflects the multinational, multicultural nature of the company's operations and market. Truthfully, there are few if any companies that are there yet. Even John Hofmeister of Shell, which is practically an icon in the literature of global HR, says "Shell is still a long ways from being multicultural at the very top. Of our top 10 people, all come from just three countries: the UK, the Netherlands, and the US."

Still, Shell's record is worth shooting for. Among the company's top 200 people, 50% are natives of countries other than those three, including countries as far flung as Malaysia and Nigeria. That's a big step up from the more typical scenario where the best local nationals can aspire to is a senior management position in their home country subsidiary.

For many companies, breaking the glass ceiling for local nationals requires changing the way they recruit, develop, and assign people from all over the world.

8. RECRUIT FROM NON-TRADITIONAL SOURCES

Companies like General Electric can lure graduates from schools like Wharton and Harvard and Massachusetts Institute of Technology. But when it decided to change the face of its global workforce, GE began looking in different places, such as the Indian Institutes of Technology.

While many international companies recruit at local universities, they are typically looking for people to fill management and technical slots in their local operations, not for people to nurture into global management positions. But when Shell hires someone straight out of school it does so with the intention of sending that person to another country for developmental purposes within a few years. That's just the beginning of career development activities for high potential people around the world.

9. ENCOURAGE THIRD-COUNTRY ASSIGNMENTS

If you were to diagram employee travel in many international companies, you'd end up with a wheel. In the middle would be the parent country, and forming a circle around it all the countries hosting local operations. The spokes branching out from parent to hosts would represent a two-way exchange of talent: parent country nationals moving out to the host countries to manage operations there or provide necessary technical support, along with some movement of host country nationals into headquarters for developmental purposes before going home to a higher management position there.

But in the leading global companies, that circle would have crisscrosses all over it, representing the movement of local nationals to operations outside their own or the parent country. Often these transfers are done to match skills with needs; so, for example, Matsushita has a German from its factory automation group working in San Francisco. Increasingly such transfers are planned to broaden the international scope of the local person, making that person more valuable to the global organization.

10. DEVELOP A WORLDWIDE TALENT DATABASE

Building and maintaining a global human resources information management system is no easy task, not even with the best computer technology. It should include every individual's education, experience, training, special skills (such as languages and technology), career goals, and development plan. Take care to research any legislation on privacy of information that may apply (see Chapter 4 under "Taking HRIS worldwide.")

Such a system is invaluable at the individual, departmental, and organizational level. Ultimately it should allow anyone with a job to fill anywhere in the world to tap into it and find the best qualified person. It should make it possible for the training and development department to assist individuals in filling gaps in their résumés. And, from a broader viewpoint, it should assist the company in assessing talent strengths and weaknesses on a worldwide organizational scale.

TO SUM IT ALL UP

There you have it: ten steps to global HR. They aren't all you ever needed to know about the subject, but they should get your HR function moving in the direction it needs to take to support your organization's global business operations.

Frequently Asked Questions (FAQs)

Q1: What does being a strategic business partner really mean?

A: See Chapter 6 under "HR as strategic business partner."

Q2: What are the most pressing issues facing global HR today?

A: See Chapter 3 under "The new century": and Chapter 6.

Q3: Is human resources really any different from personnel?

A: See Chapter 1 under "The proper role of human resources": and Chapter 3 under "The 1970s."

Q4: Why are some international companies considered more "global" than others?

A: See Chapter 2 under "The exclusive definition."

Q5: How can we put all our different country-based benefits programs online?

A: See Chapter 4 under "Benefits administration the ESS way."

Q6: How do most multinational enterprises handle compensation for expatriates?

A: See Chapter 5 under "Compensation and benefits."

Q7: Can technology really replace travel for communicating worldwide?

A: See Chapter 7 under "Nortel Networks: problem solving through virtual project teams."

Q8: Why are people in other countries so different?

A: See Chapter 8 under "Unlocking cultural differences."

Q9: What Websites should I visit to learn more about global HR?

A: See Chapter 9 under "Websites worth visiting."

Q10: How can we convince people in my company to take overseas assignments?

A: See Chapter 10 under "Make it worthwhile to take overseas assignments."

Index